THE LEADERSHIP LABYRINTH

Smyth & Helwys Publishing, Inc.
6316 Peake Road
Macon, Georgia 31210-3960
1-800-747-3016
©2005 by Smyth & Helwys Publishing
All rights reserved.
Printed in the United States of America.

The paper used in this publication meets the minimum requirements of
American National Standard for Information Sciences—
Permanence of Paper for Printed Library Materials.
ANSI Z39.48–1984. (alk. paper)

Library of Congress Cataloging-in-Publication Data

Edwards, Judson.
The Leadership Labyrinth: Negotiating the Paradoxes of Ministry / by
Judson Edwards.
p. cm.
Includes bibliographical references and index.
ISBN 1-57312-441-9 (pbk. : alk. paper)
1. Pastoral theology—Baptists. I. Title.

BV4011.3.E38 2005
253—dc22

2004018304

The Leadership Labyrinth

Negotiating the Paradoxes of Ministry

Judson Edwards

Dedication

For the people of Woodland with love and gratitude

Contents

Introduction

I nearly lost my religion one day while trying to change a flat tire. I confess to being mechanically challenged, but even *I* can usually change a flat.

This particular day, though, I couldn't get the lugs off the wheel. I grunted. I groaned. I pushed. I pulled. I beat on the lug wrench with a hammer. But the lugs wouldn't budge. Finally I gave up, left the tire unchanged, and stalked into the house, defeated.

Later that day, I vented my frustration to a friend on the phone. "Try turning the lugs the other way," he said offhandedly. Now that, I thought, was a stupid suggestion. Lugs and nuts always tighten when turned clockwise and loosen when turned counter-clockwise. Every shade-tree mechanic knows that.

Desperate, however, I gave his suggestion a try. I went back out to the garage, turned the lugs the "wrong way," and, wonder of wonders, they came loose! In a matter of moments, I had the tire off and the spare mounted. I never would have thought to "tighten" the lugs in order to loosen them unless my friend had suggested it. I just knew I was doing it the right way.

This book is about turning the "ministry lugs" the "wrong way." In my thirty years as a pastor, I have learned that being a pastor is a paradoxical profession. What seems to be the right way to do something is actually the wrong way, and what seems completely foolish is actually the best way to minister.

I have a friend who calls this approach to ministry the "Columbo Model." You might remember Columbo as the cigar-smoking, trench coat-wearing, jalopy-driving detective on the old television series. He seemed to be inept and bumbling, but his strange methods always cracked the case. Columbo went about things in exactly the "wrong way," but his unorthodox style worked. He was an effective eccentric.

This book is for pastors and church leaders who are willing to think paradoxically, who will dare to turn the ministerial lug the wrong way and see what happens. This is a book about unconventional wisdom and unorthodox ministry, but I think the ideas in this book, as strange as they seem, are actually true.

If nothing else, I hope this book will help church leaders think outside the box. We pastors are notorious for settling into our ministerial grooves and staying there for a lifetime. But a groove is just a fancy name for a rut, and occasionally we need to break out of our ruts and think new thoughts. If the paradoxical truths in these pages can shake up your thinking, get you to reexamine your approach to ministry, or even stir you up to righteous indignation about my unorthodox ways, I will consider the book a success.

And if it makes even one church leader realize again the wonder of our calling and the privilege that is ours to preach and teach and lead in the name of Christ, if it reminds even one pastor that being a pastor is supposed to be a joy (even fun!), then I will consider the book a *whopping* success.

The Leadership Paradox

The harder you try to control a group, the less control you will have.

We are awash in a sea of leadership books. For years, we've been told that leaders are supposed to mimic Rudy Giuliani, Genghis Khan, Robert E. Lee, Jack Welch, Attila the Hun, Eleanor Roosevelt, or any number of other people who have been successful leaders in history. The only constant in this sea of books is the notion that good leaders are "strong leaders." The authors of the books all tell us that leadership is not for wimps and that only no-nonsense, aggressive bulldog types should apply for leadership positions.

That presents some of us with a major dilemma: What are we non-bulldogs supposed to do? Here we are leading a church and possessing absolutely no Genghis Khan attributes. Does being mild-mannered, soft-spoken, and laid-back disqualify us for leadership? Should we promptly resign so the church can find a bulldog pastor and finally fulfill its destiny?

Since no one has yet described me as a bulldog (or a dynamic leader, come to think of it!), I feel a need to point out the first ministerial paradox every pastor needs to know: *The harder you try to control a group, the less control you will have.* The more control any person tries to assert in a group, the more reactive the group becomes. In short, "bulldog" pastors tend to divide a church and render it ineffective.

Contrary to those leadership books making best-seller lists in recent years, leadership—especially church leadership—is not about coercion. As Christian leaders, we take our cue from a Galilean peasant and not from any of the vaunted leaders extolled in books. Our management credo comes from the one who said, "The Son of Man did not come to be served, but to serve, and to give his life a ransom for many" (Matt 20:28). Let the corporate gurus be "strong leaders" if they must; pastors must be servant leaders. Our symbol of power, remember, is a cross.

Still, sometimes we forget. We read about George Patton, maybe, or Vince Lombardi and decide what our church needs is a strong leader. So we put on our military uniform or coaching garb and head to the church to lead. We bark orders, issue edicts, affect an air of confident superiority. Naively assuming that leading a church is like leading an army or a football team, we are astonished when the troops rebel or the team quits on us. It worked for Patton and Lombardi, why not us?

It doesn't work for us because this well-meaning attempt to be a strong leader actually harms the conditions needed for strong leadership in a church—trust, respect, community, and laughter.

A church needs *trust,* and a domineering pastor doesn't foster that.

A church needs *respect,* and that means the pastor treats people as equals, not as subordinates.

A church needs *community,* and that only comes when the pastor is one among many—all making decisions, all working together, all striving for the same goal.

A church needs *laughter,* and that never happens when a bulldog is on the rampage.

In *Management of the Absurd,* one of the wiser books I've read on leadership, business consultant Richard Farson writes,

> Effective leaders and managers do not regard control as the main concern. Instead, they approach situations sometimes as learners, sometimes as teachers, sometimes as both. They trust the wisdom of the group. Their strength is not in control alone, but in other qualities—passion, sensitivity, tenacity, patience, courage, firmness, enthusiasm, wonder.[1]

That last sentence provides a succinct checklist for the effective church leader:

- Passion—Am I passionate about the gospel? Passionate in my love for this church? Passionate in my love for what I do?
- Sensitivity—Can I discern the pain in a quivering voice? Sense the joy in someone's eyes? Learn to listen beneath the words?
- Tenacity—Can I "hang in there" when attendance dips, offerings plummet, and criticism comes? Do I know about "a long obedience in the same direction?"
- Patience—Do I have the capacity to love fellow sinners? Can I minister in the context of ordinary people who are blind to their foibles and flaws?

- Courage—Can I speak the truth in love? Not get offended when I don't get my way? Trust the wisdom of the group?
- Firmness—Do I know who I am and what I believe? Can I take some well-defined stands without being controlling?
- Enthusiasm—Has the good news of Christ settled in my bones? Have I laughed at least three times today? Can I remember that my relationship to God is not predicated on institutional success?
- Wonder—Do I have anything to look forward to? Am I taking time to play tennis, strum the guitar, hike in the woods, sip coffee in the bookstore?

This list, I think, defines the qualities of a "strong leader." But control? Dominance? Taking General Patton and Coach Lombardi into the sanctuary? None of that will work.

Perhaps the role model we pastors really need is the Tom Hanks character in the movie *Big*. A twelve-year-old boy wakes up one morning looking like a thirty-year-old. On the outside he's grown up, but on the inside he's still a kid.

He gets a job with a toy manufacturer and is quickly promoted to vice-president. To the amazement and chagrin of his colleagues, this man/child is praised for his leadership. His is an unlikely style that has nothing to do with dominance, certainty, or any of the other "macho" qualities we usually associate with strong leadership. His only goal is to be himself—playful, honest, lighthearted, and asker of dumb questions. Just in being himself, he leads. Others in the toy company crunch numbers and plot graphs. He just brings himself to the job, and wonderful, creative things happen.

I need to remember that example each time I steer my pickup toward the church and embark on another day of ministry. As pastor, I have the responsibility to define myself and to proclaim the truth. But leadership is not about dominance.

It is about loving what I do and being playful, honest, and real.

[1] Richard Farson, *Management of the Absurd* (New York: Simon & Schuster, 1996), 38.

The Calendar Paradox

The busier you are, the less you will accomplish.

Every so often I receive in the mail an offer that's supposed to be too good for a "busy pastor" to refuse. For a certain price, I'm offered a book of letters for all occasions so that I don't ever have to take the time to compose a letter of my own. There's a "canned" letter to send to the grief-stricken; another to send to the newcomer in town; another for someone celebrating a wedding anniversary. Since I'm so busy, I can just have my secretary make a copy of the appropriate letter on church stationery. Then I sign it, put it in the mail, and get credit for being a caring pastor.

The sad thing about that whole deal is not only its shallowness and triteness; it's the assumption that pastors are so busy they don't have time to compose a letter. The people sending me the offer for those "canned" letters think they're complimenting me when they call me a "busy pastor." Isn't it grand? I'm busy for God, busy doing the work of the ministry. Busy, busy, busy!

Eugene Peterson, for one, would beg to differ: "The word *busy* is the symptom not of commitment but of betrayal. It is not devotion but defection. The adjective *busy* set as a modifier to *pastor* should sound to our ears like *adulterous* to characterize a wife or *embezzling* to describe a banker. It is an outrageous scandal, a blasphemous affront."[1]

I know in my heart of hearts that he's right. But still my ego swells with pride when a member of my flock comments on my busyness or someone commends me for my hard work. And any time I hear a church member coming down the hall, I grab a book or pencil or start punching keys on my computer, trying my best to look busy.

Why this compulsion to be busy? Why do we pastors think it a badge of honor to be run down and worn out? Where did we get the idea that exhaustion is next to godliness?

I can only speak for myself, but my desire to look busy comes from two impulses within me:

The first has to do with my ego. I equate busyness with being important. Important people are busy people, and I *do* want to be important. I want people to look at me as a spiritual big shot, hustling for the Lord, doing big things for the kingdom. I want to look busy, in other words, because I'm keen on looking impressive to the world.

And I'm astute enough to know what is expected of me: visit all sick church members in the hospital, say the prayer at the monthly Rotary meeting, attend all church committee meetings, make sure the church bylaws are up to date, represent the church at the weekly pastors' breakfast, keep the church staff in line, plan and implement stirring worship services, get a long-range plan for the church on the drawing board, preach brilliant sermons, acts as a peacemaker in church disputes, attend all denominational conferences and conventions, contact all prospects, have a happy home life, comfort the bereaved, and be a hundred other places each month representing God and the church. That's all. Piece of cake. If I can simply do those things, people will revere me as a great pastor, and I will bask in their adulation.

I'm also astute enough to know what God expects of me: pray, preach, read, enjoy my calling, enjoy my family, dream, rest, play, write.

The problem, then, is obvious. If I give my time and energy to the first set of demands, I have no time and energy for the second set. In stepping to the world's agenda, I have no place for God's.

The second reason for my busyness relates to my theology. In spite of what I've just written about God's agenda for me, the truth is that, somewhere deep in my soul, I believe God wants me exhausted. For all of my rhetoric about grace, there is part of me geared to do works. I think I make it with God by staying busy at church.

That means my calling as a pastor is a duty, a heavy obligation that must be fulfilled. I put my hand to the pastoral plow and never look back. There is a certain element of truth to that, I suspect, but I also know it is a surefire blueprint for burnout. When I equate my status before God with my dogged performance at church, I'm treading in treacherous waters.

So, from time to time, I read the works of people like Robert Capon and get a different perspective on ministry:

Every call from God, whether into some dull line of paid work or into an excursion from such work, is a call into play—into *fun,* if you will. If you turn it into mere labor, or into a career, or into a way of making money, it will either blow up in your face, or burn you out—or both.[2]

Then he made this confession about his life as an Episcopal priest:

I have never done an honest day's work as a clergyman. In fact, I hate, despise, and avoid at least half the things clergypersons are supposed to do. I love preaching, celebrating the Eucharist, teaching, and counseling; so I have done those things just for the joy of it. I am also moderately fond of administration (which I delight in doing as quickly as possible), and I am more than a little enamored of ecclesiastical politics (which I have pursued with relish, if not success). But I have little love for writing newsletters, attending other people's meetings, paying house calls, or visiting in the hospital; so (since they are no fun), I have done as little of them as I could get away with.[3]

Capon's conclusion is a needed word to all of us serious, busy pastors: "My advice to anyone contemplating any ecclesiastical activity is, 'If you can't figure out a way of doing it for fun, do yourself and everybody else a favor and don't do it.'"[4]

I need someone like Capon to whisper in my ear from time to time that I can look for ways to have fun in my job and that I don't need to impress God with my ecclesiastical exhaustion.

When I am brutally honest, I know my busyness comes from those two sources: inflated ego and faulty theology. I'm a busy pastor because I want to impress people and because I want to impress God. I know those are silly ideas, but it's a temptation to buy into them.

The Calendar Paradox is one I have to remember constantly if I am going to be true to my true calling: *The busier you are, the less you will accomplish.* The more I give in to ego and sick theology, the less effective I will be.

Who gives me my marching orders anyway?

And what kind of God do I serve?

[1] Eugene Peterson, *The Contemplative Pastor* (Dallas: Word, 1989), 27.

[2] Robert Capon, *Health, Money, & Love* (Grand Rapids: Eerdmans, 1990), 143.

[3] Ibid., 143.

[4] Ibid., 144.

The Relationship Paradox

*The people who like you most will
be the ones you try least to please.*

I have three groups of people in my church, and my guess is that these three groups exist in every church and will be recognized by every pastor.

The first group consists of people who, when I hear their voice down the hallway, prompt me to get up from my desk and run to greet them. These are the *Energizers,* the people in my church who, by their very presence, make me feel better. They buoy my spirits, and I dare not miss an opportunity to get my energy tank refilled by their company.

The second group consists of people who, when I hear their voice down the hallway, prompt me to sit at my desk and wait for them to come my way. These are the *Regular Folks*, who usually stop at my office door and speak a friendly word as they pass by. They may not exactly buoy my spirits, but they don't demoralize me either. They certainly make up the largest group in the church.

The third group consists of people who, when I hear their voice down the hallway, prompt me to shut my door, turn off my light, and crouch in a corner of my office, hoping not to be detected. These are the *Drainers*, the people in my church who, by their very presence, sap my joy and ruin my day.

I have pondered long and hard as to what puts people in each of these groups. And I have decided that the main difference between the *Energizers* and the *Drainers* has to do with expectations. The *Energizers* have no great expectations for me. They like me as I am and accept me as I am. I'm at ease with these people because they have no agenda for me.

The *Drainers*, on the other hand, have a long list of changes I need to make. My theology is not exactly correct. I'm not a strong leader. I need to visit more diligently in the hospital. Or my church administration skills are lacking. The *Drainers* have an unspoken agenda for me (at least unspoken *to me*), and I always get the feeling when I'm around them that I'm not quite measuring up, that I've inadvertently failed them.

Since I am by nature a "pleaser," I try hard to earn the approval of these people, but my best efforts are usually in vain. The harder I try, the worse it gets . . . until I remember the Relationship Paradox: *The people who like you most will be the ones you try least to please.*

One of the most baffling paradoxes in all of life is that, in our personal relationships, effort doesn't translate into approval. Some people will like me even if I don't try to win their acceptance. Some people will never like me, no matter how hard I try to woo them. Can there be anything more frustrating than trying to win the approval of people whose approval can never be won?

When we try to meet all of the expectations of the *Drainers*, we become the "marketing character" Erich Fromm described in his book *To Have or to Be?*:

> The aim of the marketing character is complete adaptation, so as to be desirable under all conditions of the personality market. The marketing character personalities do not even have egos (as people in the nineteenth century did) to hold on to, that belong to them and that do not change. For they constantly change their egos, according to the principle "I am as you desire me."[1]

Pastors can easily become "marketing characters," selling our souls for a measure of approval. When our credo becomes "I am as you desire me," we have lost the very thing that will enable us to minister effectively: our authenticity.

I once went to the Gospels to try to determine what Jesus did with the *Drainers* in his life. I looked at the second chapter of Mark, where the ever-draining Pharisees kept dogging Jesus and criticizing his every move. I took notice of how Jesus dealt with those difficult people, and I discovered that Jesus had a three-point plan for coping with his *Drainers.*

First, Jesus retreated from his Drainers to refresh himself and seek God. Immediately after his confrontations with the Pharisees, Mark tells us that Jesus "withdrew with his disciples to the lake" (3:7). It is impossible to deal with *Drainers* all the time. We will inevitably burn out and run down. Jesus wisely used the "rhythm of renewal" in his life and, after his draining time of conflict with the religious leaders, escaped for a time of rest. Like all of us, he needed to get his battery recharged.

Tim Hansel, in his book *When I Relax I Feel Guilty*, described his ministerial fatigue like this:

> Days were not lived but endured. I was exhausted trying to be a hope constantly rekindled for others, straining to live up to their images of me. I had worked

hard to develop a reputation as one who was concerned, available, and involved—now I was being tyrannized by it. Often I was more at peace in the eyes of others than in my own.[2]

When we neglect the rhythm of renewal, Hansel's words will be our testimony too. Often we need to follow Jesus' pattern and get away for a while, to retreat from ecclesiastical worries and ministerial facades and get in touch with who we really are. And get in touch again with God.

Second, Jesus balanced his Drainers with his Energizers. I had never noticed before the timing of Jesus' calling of the twelve apostles. It was right after his draining encounter with the Pharisees that "Jesus went up on a mountainside and called to him those he wanted, and they came to him. He appointed twelve that they might be with him" (3:13).

Jesus called out these twelve men right after dealing with difficult people. He knew he was going to need some *Energizers* in his life, people who would share his dreams and stoke his coals. Those twelve men might not have lived up to their potential as *Energizers*, but that was to be their purpose. Sure, they were to learn from Jesus. But they were also supposed to energize him and help him keep his dream alive. We have to have those people in our lives. We have to have people who prompt us to run down the hallway so we can bask in their delight. Blessed indeed are pastors whose *Energizers* outnumber their *Drainers*.

Third, Jesus didn't let the Drainers deter him from his plan and purpose. After all of this—the conflict with the Pharisees, the attempted getaway to renew himself, and the choosing of the Twelve—Jesus then had to grapple with a man possessed by a demon (3:20ff).

What would he do, face to face with the Evil One? Jesus confronted the situation head-on and healed the man. Maybe it's more instructive to notice what Jesus *didn't* do. He *didn't* get intimidated by the Pharisees' criticism. He *didn't* shrink from doing what he was called to do. And he *didn't* quit loving people. He simply kept "doing his thing." True to form, his *Drainers* slandered him and accused him of being demon-possessed himself.

It is tempting to let *Drainers* ruin our lives. Our attempts to be acceptable can become all-consuming: "Why are they mad at me? What can I do to win their approval? Why are they always so critical?" Jesus never got caught up in any of that. He just kept on loving, forgiving, healing, and serving God.

Don't misunderstand. In spite of his strategy, Jesus never did get rid of his *Drainers*. Even though he had the rhythm of renewal and withdrew from time to time, even though he tried to circle up some *Energizers* to help him, and even though he kept on doing what he was called to do, he still had to contend with opposition and criticizers all of his life.

So, possibly, will we. No one ever said ministry would be an easy job. But it helps make things bearable to remember the Relationship Paradox, that even our finest efforts can't win some people's applause, and even our most mediocre performances can't keep some people from applauding us.

Go figure. The only people we can really please are the ones we don't have to work hard to please.

I like the analogy Richard Bach uses in his book, *Illusions*:

Well. . . . we're magnets, aren't we? Not magnets. We're iron, wrapped in copper wire, and whenever we want to magnetize ourselves we can. Pour our inner voltage through the wire, we can attract whatever we want to attract. A magnet is not anxious about how it works. It is itself, and by its nature draws some things and leaves others untouched.[3]

If our life map says everyone will be attracted to us, it is time to update the map. As one of my acquaintances puts it, "It is not appointed to one person to ring everybody's bell."

I had to come to grips with that myself years ago. Not everyone will like my preaching. I know that's hard to believe, but it's true. Not everyone will buy my books. Not everyone will find my personality scintillating.

But—and here's the good news in the Relationship Paradox—some will! I *will* influence some people because they like my message, my style, my *me*. On surprisingly frequent occasions, the magnet will do its natural work.

[1] Erich Fromm, *To Have or to Be?* (New York: Harper & Row, 1976), 148.

[2] Tim Hansel, *When I Relax I Feel Guilty* (Elgin IL: David C. Cook, 1979), 22.

[3] Richard Bach, *Illusions* (New York: Dell, 1977), 146.

The Anxiety Paradox

The less you worry about the church, the better it will do.

Edwin Friedman was a Jewish rabbi and family therapist who, in 1985, wrote a book titled *Generation to Generation*. The book was an attempt to take "family systems theory" and apply it to churches and synagogues. Friedman took his knowledge of family systems and his experience as the leader of a synagogue and combined them into one book.

The book is primarily about leadership in a religious system. Friedman detailed how religious systems work and how a person can be an effective leader in a church or synagogue. One of the essential ingredients for leadership, Friedman said, is the capacity to be a "non-anxious presence":

> The capacity of members of the clergy to contain their own anxiety regarding congregational matters, both those related to them, as well as those where they become the identified focus, may be the most significant capability in their arsenal. Not only can such capacity enable religious leaders to be more clear-headed about solutions and more adroit in triangles, but, because of the systemic effect that a leader's functioning always has on an entire organism, a non-anxious presence will modify anxiety throughout the entire congregation.[1]

Friedman then drew an electrical analogy and said leaders can function like transformers in an electrical circuit:

> To the extent we are anxious ourselves, then, when anxiety in the congregation permeates our being, it becomes potentiated and feeds back into the congregational family at a much higher voltage. But to the extent we can recognize and contain our own anxiety, then we function as step-down transformers, or perhaps circuit breakers. In that case, our presence, far from escalating emotional potential, actually serves to diminish its "zapping" effect.[2]

In essence, the more anxious the leader, the more anxious the system. Thus the Anxiety Paradox: *The less you worry about the church, the better it will do.*

When I first read Friedman's book years ago, I was immediately struck with the truth of many of his ideas, especially this concept of the "non-anxious presence." But I was also reminded of an old episode of the *Andy Griffith Show.* In this particular episode, Sheriff Andy Taylor and Deputy Barney Fife were getting ready to investigate a haunted house. Barney, in a rare moment of candor, confessed to Andy that he was scared to death to go in the house. Andy tried to reassure him: "Barney, just remember, there's nothing to fear but fear itself." But Barney wasn't comforted. He got a panicked look on his face and said, "But, Andy, that's exactly what I have—fear itself!"

I thought about that old Andy Griffith episode because I felt like Barney after I read Friedman. Sure, a leader should be a non-anxious presence. But what if you have anxiety itself? What if just saying you should be non-anxious doesn't make it so? How can a chronically anxious pastor suddenly become a "non-anxious presence"?

Anyone who has been in church work more than a week knows there is plenty to be anxious about. I often liken church work to juggling. The church leader is asked to keep a dozen balls in the air at the same time (or is it a hundred?). Just about the time you get the preschool department "ball" spiffed up and running smoothly, the youth department "ball" crashes to the ground. And so you turn your efforts to the youth ministry and start making progress there when the church air conditioner craters. So you raise money for a new air conditioner and things start looking pretty favorable when two staff members suddenly decide they can't stand each other. So you turn your attention to repairing that relationship when . . . well, you know what I'm talking about.

Church work is trying to keep all the balls in the air but knowing that it will never, ever happen.

What that means, of course, is that church work produces a ton of anxiety. We're always trying to juggle the balls properly, but they keep falling to the ground, and we typically stay both anxious and frustrated. It makes no one happy when balls keep getting dropped.

I wish I could give you a simple solution to our shared anxiety problem, but I want instead to carom over to a passage in the Old Testament. It is a passage that has helped me as I have tried to deal with my own anxiety, and I hope it will help you too.

It is the story in 2 Kings 6 in which the servant of the prophet Elisha discovers he has surprising resources on his side—enough resources, in fact, to calm his fear and give him confidence. This servant woke up one morning and saw to his dismay that the enemy had encircled the town where he and his master Elisha had spent the night. He was terrified and went to Elisha with one simple question: "Oh, my Lord, what shall we do?"

Elisha answered him calmly, "Don't be afraid. Those who are with us are more than those who are with them."

Then Elisha prayed and asked God to open the servant's eyes so that he could see reality as it truly was.

The text says, "Then the LORD opened the servant's eyes, and he looked and saw the hills full of horses and chariots of fire all around Elisha" (2 Kgs 6:17).

That story speaks to me because many days I *am* that servant. Some mornings when I awaken, stroll to the French doors in our den, and look out to see what a new day brings, I see the enemy. The enemy assumes different poses, but he shows up with regularity.

Sometimes the enemy assumes the shape of a person in the church who is upset with me.

Sometimes the enemy is sagging attendance or a budget deficit.

Sometimes the enemy is personal laziness, an unwillingness to roll up my sleeves and tackle an unpleasant situation.

Quite often, the enemy encircling my house is staleness, boredom, a lack of passion for doing the tasks I'm supposed to do.

What I try to remind myself, as my anxiety soars in the face of those enemies, is that I have more than enough resources to face the day with passion and zest. Those who are with me are more than those who are with them. On those mornings, when I survey the enemy encircling my home and heart, I try to see the horses and chariots of fire all around me.

I remember:

- a wife and two grown children who love me and will do anything in the world for me.
- hundreds of books that inspire and instruct me, books that give me warmth when the world grows cold.
- a church brimming with kind and creative souls who let me be their pastor.
- friends who will meet me for lunch whenever I need them and others who are just a phone call away.
- thirty years of experience as a pastor. I have looked out this same window many times, seen these same formidable enemies, and am still standing, still triumphant.
- a strong sense of calling to be in this place. I trust that I am exactly where God wants me to be.

• God. Best of all, I have an unfathomable, gracious, relentless God who has sustained me all of my days and, I trust, will continue to sustain and love me until the end of my life. With the apostle Paul I sometimes find myself singing, "If God is for me, who can be against me?" (Rom 8:31).

So on those mornings when the enemy appears especially ferocious and my stomach churns with anxiety, I remember these "horses and chariots of fire" and, with all of the faith I can muster, head to the church to be a pastor-leader another day.

Turn on the computer.

Pour myself a cup of coffee.

Greet my staff as they arrive.

And remember the wonderfully liberating Anxiety Paradox: The less I worry about what goes on around here, the better things will go.

[1] Edwin Friedman, *Generation to Generation* (New York: Guilford, 1985), 208.

[2] Ibid., 208-209.

The Stewardship Paradox

*The more you preach about
money, the less you will receive.*

When our church budget is running at a deficit and people are starting to get nervous, the Finance Committee will usually suggest that I need to preach more sermons on stewardship. I typically mumble a short response—something to the effect that I actually preach quite a bit about stewardship—but then agree to address the issue again soon. When the stewardship issue surfaces next time, here's what I think I will say (or *should* say) to the Finance Committee:

There are two kinds of stewardship sermons.

One is the kind we often hear on radio and television and sometimes in other churches. These sermons follow a general theme: "Our church is behind in its budget giving, and you need to reach deeper and give more sacrificially. If you continue in your greedy, selfish ways, this church is going down the drain. We don't want that to happen, do we? Besides that, the Bible has a lot to say about money and tithing and how it's the Christian's duty to give. The good news, though, is that we can't outgive God. If we will open our hearts and our wallets, God will pour out his favor upon us and shower us with blessings."

If that is your definition of a stewardship sermon, I have never preached a stewardship sermon in my life. Not one. And frankly, I have no plans to preach a sermon like that any time soon.

The second kind of stewardship sermon is the kind that goes something like this: "All the things that matter—our time, relationships, health, possessions, the created order, and so on—are gifts from a good God. We are, of all people, most blessed. And since we are so blessed, our calling as followers of Jesus is to share what we have with others. Out of a glad and generous spirit, we are to give freely of our money and possessions, to invest our treasures in people. Freely we have received; freely we give. A sure measure of our Christian maturity is the amount of joy we have in giving."

If that is your definition of a stewardship sermon, I have preached many of them and will be happy to preach many more. If stewardship is about receiving the grace of God and then being gracious in our relationships, that is one of the main themes of my preaching.

But that is a more indirect way to approach the subject of stewardship, and some might find it too indirect. They think I should spell it out more clearly, talk about the budget from the pulpit, and keep passing the plate until we make up the deficit. They think a good stewardship sermon hits people over the head and makes them feel guilty.

I, on the other hand, firmly believe in the Stewardship Paradox: *The more you preach about money, the less you will receive.* I think people are smart enough not to want to be hit over the head. I think people will give if they understand stewardship from a biblical perspective. Giving flows out of grace, not guilt, and the more grace we put on people the more generous they become. Conversely, the more guilt we put on people, the more bitter and resistant they become.

Any time I think about preaching a stewardship sermon, I do so with four truths in the back of my mind:

First, I am speaking mostly to church people who have sat through more stewardship sermons than they care to recall. It bears remembering, I think, that people come to church with a history. Many of the people in our church come with a fine history of Christian discipleship. But they also come with a history of past sermons that harangued them for their lack of generosity. They come to church, in short, with a history loaded with guilt about their giving. Why add to that pile of guilt? Why not try a different tack—giving not as obligation but as celebration? Why not take Paul's admonition seriously and try to produce a bunch of cheerful givers?

Second, I am speaking to people who come to church out of a culture of salesmanship and manipulation. To put it bluntly, people are sick and tired of telemarketers, slick salespeople, and anyone else wanting their money and time. The "hard sell" has fallen on hard times. People are growing increasingly cynical of "good causes," and justifiably so. I steadfastly refuse to turn the church into another institution wanting people's allegiance and money. Church ought to be the one place in a pressured, manipulated society where people are not pressured or manipulated. However we choose to stress stewardship in our church, we must avoid at all costs techniques and programs borrowed from a sales-oriented society. Jesus deserves better, and so do his people.

Third, it is entirely possible that someone might choose to support God's work and not give to our church. I find it hard to believe, but it is possible. I would like to think that people—especially our own church members—would look at the worship and ministries of our church and decide that our church is absolutely the best place to invest their money to further God's kingdom. But I am realistic enough to admit that someone might come to a different conclusion. Some people might decide that another ministry is a better spiritual investment for their dollar. I just need to declare the stewardship-by-grace idea as clearly as I can and then let people decide how and where to give. I also have to remind myself, from time to time, that the kingdom of God is bigger than our little church.

Fourth, indirect communication is the most effective way to persuade people. That idea was proposed by Soren Kierkegaard in the mid-1800s, but it strikes me as especially true for modern communicators. Kierkegaard said, "To thunder is no longer of any avail; it only embitters men."[1] He believed the best way to communicate the gospel, especially to people who have already heard it, is to do so indirectly. He used this simple analogy: "In sawing wood it is important not to press down too hard on the saw; the lighter the pressure exerted by the sawyer, the better the saw operates. If a man were to press down with all his strength, he would no longer be able to saw at all."[2] When it comes to stewardship sermons, that is especially true. In a cynical, jaded culture, the light touch will be the most effective touch.

Those four ideas hover in the background of every sermon I preach on money and giving, and they prompt me to reaffirm the truth of the Stewardship Paradox. Stewardship needs to be taught, but from a stance of grace and with the clear understanding that the lighter the pressure from the preacher, the better the sermon will persuade.

Mark Twain once told about attending church and hearing the preacher make a plea for money. At first, Twain said, he wanted to give $50. But the longer the preacher preached, the less he wanted to give. When at the end of the hour-long sermon the offering plates were passed, Twain said he reached in and helped himself to a quarter.

That story is typical Twain. It's got a barbed humor that lampoons us with the truth. And the truth is: Too much talk about money turns off potential givers.

Well, Finance Committee, I'm sorry I've used up all of your committee time with my ramblings about stewardship sermons. I guess you hit my "hot button."

Like you, I believe we need to preach and teach on stewardship. I just want to do it in the most effective and biblical way possible.

---

[1] Quoted in Fred B. Craddock, *Overhearing the Gospel* (Nashville: Abingdon, 1978), 84.

[2] Ibid., 115.

The Preaching Paradox

The more you preach, the less you will have to say.

The Preaching Paradox can be interpreted in two ways, but either way you interpret it, it makes sense.

One way to think of the Preaching Paradox is to apply it to an individual sermon on a particular Sunday morning: the more you preach—the longer you preach that Sunday—the less effective your sermon will be. From this perspective, the Preaching Paradox is an invitation to shorter sermons.

The other way to think of the Preaching Paradox is to apply it to ministerial longevity: the longer you are in the ministry and the more sermons you preach over time, the less you will have to say. From this angle, the Preaching Paradox says that as we grow old, we can also grow tired, jaded, bored, cynical, or lifeless. A life of saying words from the pulpit can leave us without much to say. From this perspective, the Preaching Paradox is an invitation to personal renewal, to finding ways to keep the "fire" alive within us.

Both interpretations of the Preaching Paradox are valid, and both bear pondering.

From the first angle, the paradox calls us to look at the length of our sermons. We preachers who love to hear the sound of our own voices, need to consider the remote possibility that the longer we talk, the less effectively we will communicate. When it comes to effective communication, brevity is key. I say that for three reasons:

First, the times demand it. We live in a day of hurry and frenzy. People are on the move, and attention spans seem to be shrinking. Long-winded orations from the pulpit simply will not reach this crowd.

I once clipped from a magazine a poem I thought captured the frenetic pace of our culture:

This is the age
Of the half-read page
And the quick hash
And the mad dash
The bright night
With the nerves tight
The plane hop
With the brief stop
The lamp tan
In a short span
The big shot
In a good spot
And the brain strain
And the heart pain
And the cat naps
Till the spring snaps
And the fun's done.[1]

Imagine my surprise when I noticed that a poet named Virginia Brasier penned the poem in 1949. That "contemporary" snapshot of our culture is more than fifty years old!

But if brains were strained, hearts were pained, and springs were snapping fifty years ago, the current scene is even worse. Tension is high, people are preoccupied, and lengthy speech—whether written or spoken—is generally ignored. This is the time for a brief word "fitly spoken." Sermons need to be distilled truth, the word condensed to its essence. We are shooting at moving targets today, and the best chance we have of actually hitting those targets is to fire fast, precise bullets at them.

Second, Jesus modeled it. Brevity makes sense because Jesus gave us an eloquent example that when it comes to talking about God, less is better. He was a master of the brief word—the one-line zinger, the short parable stuffed with meaning, the rhetorical question that prompted people to think. Even the brilliant Sermon on the Mount in Matthew could have been spoken in less than fifteen minutes.

The poet Marianne Moore once commented that "expanded explanation tends to spoil the lion's leap."[2] Jesus never "spoiled the lion's leap" by talking too much. In contrast to the other preachers of his day, he spoke with authority. When he spoke of God, he spoke simply, directly, and briefly. And so should we.

Third, urgency requires it. There is a law of physics that states "to compress is to heat." That applies to preaching as well. The more we can compress biblical truth, the more "heat" it will have.

Think for a moment about an emergency situation when an urgent word needs to be sounded. Maybe a house is on fire, and you must get word to the people inside. Do you dawdle, amble to the house, ponder possible causes of the fire, and construct a long oration to deliver once you arrive? No! You rush to the house and yell "Fire!" at the top of your lungs. The brevity of the message is crucial to the urgency of the threat.

And so it is in preaching. When we overtalk the Bible, we remove the urgency from our message. We're like the person fashioning a carefully-worded document while the house burns. Better to run into the sanctuary and yell "Fire!"

Anthony Trollope was a nineteenth-century novelist who sometimes played the role of clergy-critic in his novels. In one of them, *Barchester Towers*, he launched this attack, which is both dated and highly relevant:

> There is, perhaps, no greater hardship at present inflicted on mankind in civilized and free countries than the necessity of listening to sermons. No one but a preaching clergyman has, in these realms, the power of compelling an audience to sit silent and be tormented. No one but a preaching clergyman can revel in platitudes, truisms and untruisms, and yet receive, as his undisputed privilege, the same respectful demeanour as though words of impassioned eloquence, or persuasive logic, fell from his lips.

Trollope then goes on to say that public worship is a good thing, something to be desired, "but we desire also that we may do so without an amount of tedium which ordinary human nature cannot endure with patience." His fervent request of preachers is "that we may be able to leave the house of God without that anxious longing for escape which is the common consequence of common sermons."[3]

His point, sadly, is well taken. But wouldn't it be fine if we preachers could speak so succinctly and capture the gospel so sharply that worshipers would have not a longing for escape, but a longing for more?

That, then, is the first way of thinking about the Preaching Paradox. The longer we preach, the less we will communicate. This first interpretation offers us an invitation to be brief when we speak of holy things.

The second possible interpretation of the Preaching Paradox deserves our consideration too—especially those of us who have been serving as pastors for years. The paradox we're dealing with is that our experience hasn't made our preaching easier; it has made it harder. As we have gotten older, wiser, and less idealistic, we have less to say now than we did in our naïve younger days. Besides that, we've grown a bit weary of hearing our own pontifications about God and wish we could shut up for a while.

Our dilemma is captured well by a quote from Diadochus of Photiki that Henri Nouwen uses in his book, *The Way of the Heart*: "When the door of the steambath is continually left open, the heat inside rapidly escapes through it; likewise the soul, in its desire to say many things, dissipates its remembrance of God through the door of speech, even though everything it says may be good."[4]

For all of these years that we have been preaching, the door of our steambath has been left open, and the heat inside has gradually dissipated. We've arrived at mid-life (or later), seasoned, competent . . . and cold. More Sundays than we care to admit, we serve lukewarm leftovers to hungry searchers.

Nouwen commented on our plight this way: "It is not so strange that many ministers have become burnt-out cases, people who say many words and share many experiences, but in whom the fire of God's Spirit has died and from whom not much more comes forth than their own boring, petty ideas and feelings."[5]

The pressing question then becomes: "So what do we do about it?" It's one thing to sense the heat dissipating; it's another thing altogether to rekindle the flame. How do "experienced preachers" restore their passion?

I don't think there is a tried-and-true formula for preacher-renewal. Each pastor must decide for himself or herself how to restore the fire. Like snowflakes and fingerprints, strategies of personal revival are unique to each individual.

At least for me, renewal has something to do with remembering my identity as a pastor. When I forget who I am, who I'm called to be, I inevitably sink into lethargy. But when I remember my calling—I'm a pastor, not the CEO of a religious business, not a salesman, not a dog-and-pony show, not a nice guy who prays at Kiwanis meetings, and not a fix-it man who can solve people's problems—I am able to stoke the coals in my soul.

When I first moved to my current church, I wrote a free-verse poem and put it in my desk drawer. Some days, when I feel the flames being doused, I pull out this poem and remember again who I am.

Memo for a Monday Morning
Remember:
    There is a Reality deeper, or higher, than
    How many people showed up for church yesterday
    Or how large the offering was.

Remember:

> There is a Reality deeper, or higher, than
> How many people joined your church yesterday
> Or how the building program is progressing.

Remember:

> There is a Reality deeper, or higher, than
> How well you preached yesterday
> Or how many compliments you received.

Remember:

> There is a Reality deeper, or higher, than
> Your plans and schemes for institutional success
> Or personal glory.

Remember:

> There is God, the One in whom you live and move
> And have your being
> The One who called you and will bless you in spite of your failures.

Remember:

> Your job is to trust and be faithful
> And laugh and relax,
> To believe Romans 8:28 is actually true.

Remember:

> Your job is to model a different way of thinking
> For your people,
> To treat success lightly and fidelity seriously.

And always remember:

> The machinery of institutionalism can grind the life out of you
> And rob you of your joy
> And your calling.

THIS IS THE DAY THE LORD HAS MADE. WE WILL REJOICE AND BE GLAD IN IT.

I wrote that less-than-brilliant poem to remind myself that I am here to do more than oversee an institution; I am here to model a different way of living and to challenge others to do the same. As long as I can remember that, the fire stays alive within me.

Vincent Van Gogh, the great Dutch painter, once said:

There may be a great fire in your soul, yet no one ever comes to warm himself at it, and the passersby only see a wisp of smoke coming through the chimney, and go along their way. Look here, now what must be done? Must one tend the inner fire, have salt in one-self, wait patiently yet with how much impatience for the hour when somebody will come and sit down—maybe to stay? Let him who believes in God wait for the hour that will come sooner or later.[6]

That is the challenge confronting us in the second interpretation of the Preaching Paradox. Though we are getting older and it's all too easy for the fire to dissipate, we find ways to tend the inner fire, to have salt in ourselves.

And we trust that at least a few people—maybe not the masses, but a few—will come and sit down and be warmed by our fire.

[1] Virginia Brasier, "Time of the Mad Atom," reprinted from *The Saturday Evening Post* (28 May 1949), 72.

[2] Marianne Moore, *Predilections* (New York: Viking, 1955), 3.

[3] Anthony Trollope, *Barchester Towers* (New York: Doubleday, 1945), 49-50.

[4] Henri Nouwen, *The Way of the Heart* (New York: Ballantine, 1981), 37-38.

[5] Ibid., 39.

[6] Quoted in Nouwen, *The Way of the Heart*, 39.

The Negotiation Paradox

The most serious issues cannot be handled seriously.

The church traffics in the "big issues" of life. No small concerns or trivial pursuits for us. We're all about the formidable S's—Sin, Salvation, Stewardship, Servanthood, Sickness, and Sorrow. Those of us who lead churches are well aware that we handle these grave issues on a weekly, if not daily, basis.

Our tendency, naturally, is to approach these grave issues Seriously. Serious issues demand Serious attitudes, Serious discussions, Serious prayers. Every day we march to church with our "game faces on," ready to be Serious.

Sadly, what this does is create an atmosphere of Seriousness and Sobriety that is the antithesis to good news. The writer Robert Louis Stevenson purportedly wrote in his journal one day, "Wonders of wonders! I have been to church today and am not depressed." When we approach those formidable S's with our Serious game face on, everyone gets depressed—including us!

And our attempts to handle serious issues seriously actually set in motion a destructive cycle that moves the church not toward commitment, but toward apathy. Edwin Friedman wrote:

> Seriousness can be destructive. Seriousness is more than an attitude; it is a total orientation, a way of thinking embedded in constant, chronic anxiety. It is characterized by a lack of flexibility in response, a narrow repertoire of approaches, persistent efforts to try harder, an inability to change direction, and a loss of perspective and concentrated focus.[1]

Our good-intentioned efforts to handle serious issues seriously only serves to perpetuate a chronically-anxious system that leaves everyone feeling a little bit like Longfellow. We can get to the point where we're surprised when we return from a church committee meeting, or even a worship service, and don't feel depressed.

Stuck in seriousness, we've grown accustomed to church being a depressing experience.

That's why the Negotiation Paradox needs to be in our minds (and in our committee meetings and worship services!): *The most serious issues cannot be handled seriously.*

As formidable as the S's are, they do not yield to a serious approach. They are better approached playfully, quizzically, indirectly, and mysteriously. If we can ever learn to hand the serious S's in those ways, we might succeed in making the gospel good news again.

But handling the big S's in those ways does not come naturally, especially if you are by nature a "serious person." Some years ago, in another book, I confessed my natural tendency to be a rather serious stick-in-the-mud:

> I am not by nature a jolly good fellow. I am the shy, nervous type that likes solitude and privacy. Give me a choice between a crowd and a good book, and I will always choose the latter. No one has ever accused me of being the life of any party.
>
> My idea of a good time is running three miles a day in the Texas heat. While normal people are eating chips and dip, and watching a ball game on television in an air-conditioned living room, I am jogging through the subdivision, panting and sweating with glee.
>
> You get the picture. I tend to be a circumspect, antiseptic party-pooper. I preach joy better than I live it. Indeed, I write about the abundant life better than I live it too.[2]

When that is your normal way of approaching life, the Negotiation Paradox does not come easy. But I have learned through the years that seriousness is a dead-end street. Dealing with serious issues seriously perpetuates a negative cycle and leads to depression.

So, to counter my inclination toward too much seriousness, I try to remember the following four truths:

First, seriousness promotes stuck-ness. When Friedman said that a serious attitude "is characterized by a lack of flexibility in response, a narrow repertoire of approaches, persistent efforts to try harder, an inability to change direction, and a loss of perspective and concentrated focus," he was really saying that seriousness promotes stuck-ness. When we get serious, we lose the capacity to think "outside the box." Serious church leaders can no longer dream dreams and see visions.

Tom Peters, in his book *The Pursuit of WOW!*, told of a small company that adopted the following statement as one of its goals: "Have a collegial, supportive, yeasty, zany, laughter-filled environment where folks support one another, and politics is as absent as it can be in a human (i.e., imperfect) enterprise."[3] Wouldn't that be a fine standard for churches to establish? Wouldn't we be brighter light and zestier salt if we had a "collegial, supportive, yeasty, zany, laughter-filled" environment in our churches?

Granted, things would have to change considerably for that to happen. Most churches do fairly well in the "collegial, supportive" part of that statement but fail miserably in the "yeasty, zany, laughter-filled" part. But any church that wants to move, change, and explore is going to have to be yeasty, zany, and laughter-filled. Until we get out of our seriousness, we are doomed to staying stuck in sameness.

Second, hairballs are made to be orbited. A writer named Gordon McKenzie has written a yeasty, zany, laughter-filled book titled *Orbiting the Giant Hairball.* The subtitle of the book is "A Corporate Fool's Guide to Surviving with Grace." It could also be subtitled "A Pastor's Guide to Surviving with Grace." See if any of this sounds anything like the church you serve:

> Every new policy is another hair for the Hairball. Hairs are never taken away, only added. Even frequent reorganizations have failed to remove hairs (people, sometimes; hairs, never). Quite the contrary, each reorganization seems to add a *whole new layer* of hairs. The Hairball grows enormous.
>
> With the increase in the Hairball's mass comes a corresponding increase in the Hairball's gravity. There is such a thing as Corporate Gravity. As in the world of physics, so too in the corporate world: *The gravitational pull a body exerts increases as the mass of that body increases.* And, like physical gravity, it is the nature of Corporate Gravity to suck everything into the mass—in this case, into the mass of Corporate Normalcy.
>
> The trouble with this is that Corporate Normalcy derives from and is dedicated to past realities and past successes. There is no room in the Hairball of Corporate Normalcy for original thinking or primary creativity. Resynthesizing *past* successes is the habit of the Hairball.[4]

Doesn't that have a familiar ring to it? We have *Ecclesiastical Gravity* and *Ecclesiastical Normalcy,* too, and most definitely we have our fair share of *Ecclesiastical Hairballs.*

In fact, there is a foolproof way to determine how serious and stuck our church is: if we are focused on bylaws, policies, committee meetings and reports, staff evaluations, financial data, and other institutional concerns, we are probably both serious and stuck. We are focused more on *paper* than *people.*

Certainly, those institutional things must be tended, and I'm not pretending the modern church is not an institution. I just know that bylaws, policies, and reports don't produce energy and life. They only add to the Hairball that eventually grows so large it takes all of our time just to maintain it. And they keep us from "original thinking and primary creativity."

Third, the envelope is just as important as the letter. Linguistics experts tell us that communication involves two factors: the *message* and the *metamessage*. The message is the content of the communication; the metamessage is the process by which the communication is delivered. The message is the picture; the metamessage is the frame around the picture. The message is the letter; the metamessage is the envelope in which the letter is delivered.

From my experience, the envelope is every bit as vital as the letter. Those of us who preach weekly know the importance of the metamessage. We might have a brilliant sermon prepared for this particular Sunday. We have studied, prayed, and, wonder of wonders, everything has come together perfectly. We have conjured a homiletical masterpiece. The message, we feel confident, will be superb. But we also know that there are many other factors at work in communicating that message. Our homiletical masterpiece can still fall as flat as a day-old pancake if the metamessages don't fall in line too.

What if we catch a cold between now and Sunday and have to sniffle our way through the sermon? What if we have a spat with our spouse on the way to church and enter the pulpit in a bad humor? What if the sound system malfunctions? What if the air conditioner goes out and people are sweltering? What if our words say Grace but our body language and tone of voice say Law? What if the music on Sunday is off-key and distracting?

None of those are *content* issues; they are *process* issues. But process is as crucial as content. When you think about all of the things that have to happen for effective communication to take place, we ought to do cartwheels every time we preach a sermon that actually connects.

The envelope is as important as the letter. That has huge implications for the way we "do church." We can have a church council meeting about youth policies in an envelope that is serious, sober, and strident. Or we can have a church council meeting about youth policies in an envelope that is "collegial, supportive, yeasty, zany, and laughter-filled."

The results of that council meeting will be determined not so much by the content to be discussed as by the emotional processes used to discuss that content. A meeting in a serious, sober, strident setting will inevitably produce bad results. A meeting in a zany, laughter-filled setting will inevitably produce new ideas and closer relationships. Same topic in both meetings, same letter, but very different envelopes—and very different results.

I've become so aware of the emotional process at work in meetings that I now dislike meeting people in my office at church and try to avoid meeting there whenever possible. When someone calls requesting a meeting with me, I nearly always suggest we get a cup of coffee at a local café or that we huddle over lunch. Meeting in my office says, "This is direct, personal, intimidating, and serious." Meeting elsewhere says, "This is indirect, casual, friendly, and fun." I like the second envelope much better.

If we are sensitive and creative, there are many "friendly envelopes" we can use at church to enhance communication—and to enhance relationships.

Fourth, playfulness is magical. When I talk about not treating serious issues seriously, I am not advocating that the pastor become a clown (though using humor is a fine way to be playful). I'm not suggesting that we buy joke books or that we decorate our study with "Three Stooges" wallpaper (though I do have an M&M dispenser on my desk to make my study less intimidating). I'm simply saying that seriousness creates a stifling atmosphere that is deadly for churches.

Playfulness, on the other hand, creates an atmosphere that is energizing for churches. Playfulness is an attitude of casual joy that becomes contagious. Any time a committee meeting takes on a playful tone, good things are going to happen. Any time a counseling session moves in the direction of playfulness, a breakthrough is possible. Any time a Sunday school class is zany and laughter-filled, the members of the class might be on the verge of learning something new. And let's even go far enough to say that any time we can move beyond seriousness in our worship, someone present just might meet the Lord of the Dance that Sunday.

Earlier I mentioned the "Columbo Model" of pastoring, and one reason he is such a good role model is his playfulness. Columbo's "envelope" is a playful one. True, he's dealing with murder and mayhem, but the envelope is not serious. Columbo shows up in an old jalopy, wearing rumpled clothes, smoking a cigar, looking befuddled. No one takes him "seriously," but his lack of seriousness makes him a good detective. He's off-the-wall, creative, and wise, and it all comes packaged in a playful envelope.

But Columbo is not our best model for playfulness. Our best model is Jesus. Think about it: He made his entrance into the world as a fragile baby in a bed of straw. He grew up in a carpenter's home and looks to all the world like a Nazarene hayseed. He chose twelve common men to be his followers. He hung out with nonreligious types, even known sinners. He told quirky stories about coins and sheep and seeds. He went to parties and had a good time. He frustrated the righteous, religious people of his day by refusing to practice the legalistic rituals they espoused. He died on a cross between two crooks and then danced out of the tomb a free man.

I ask you: Does that sound like a respectable Messiah to you? It certainly wasn't the kind of Messiah anyone was expecting. Jesus was too paradoxical and playful to be anybody's idea of a Messiah. But, of course, we believe he was. And he stands as our best model for being at least a little paradoxical and playful ourselves.

The four ideas I've mentioned in this chapter are now lodged in my mind, but sometimes I forget them and revert to my serious, sober self. When I forget them, I get real serious. . .and real *stuck*. I start focusing on Hairballs. I forget how important the "envelope" always is. And I lose my playfulness and the sense of adventure playfulness always brings. In short, I become a serious Baptist pastor.

But when I remember that *the most serious issues cannot be handled seriously* and the four ideas that go with that paradox, I can sit loose and enjoy being a pastor. Unlike Stevenson, I can go to church and expect to have a good time.

[1] Edwin Friedman, *Generation to Generation* (New York: Guilford, 1985), 50.

[2] Judson Edwards, *Regaining Control of Your Life* (Minneapolis: Bethany House, 1989), 8.

[3] Tom Peters, *The Pursuit of WOW!* (New York: Vintage Books, 1994), 18.

[4] Gordon McKenzie, *Orbiting the Giant Hairball* (New York: Viking, 1996), 31.

The Learning Paradox

You will only learn more of what you already know.

I take Thursdays off from my church duties and try to use that day to relax and have fun. I have a fairly standard regimen each Thursday that includes at least the following activities: tennis in the morning, grocery shopping with Sherry, lunch out, making our soup of the week, and a trip to the bookstore to browse books and sip coffee. Needless to say, Thursday is my favorite day of the week.

On those Thursday jaunts to the bookstore, I'm prowling for knowledge. I want to find books that challenge me, inspire me, entertain me, and keep me on the cutting edge of the latest information. I like to think of myself as a person still in process, still hungry to learn new truth.

But when I enter the bookstore each Thursday, I've noticed that I have a fairly standard regimen there too. I peruse the new books at the front of the store, then head to the religion section to forage there. Next, depending on my mood, I saunter over to the fiction section, the business section, or the sociology/current affairs section. I have never once sauntered intentionally in the direction of books on physics, astronomy, archery, computers, or photography. Certainly those are all valid concerns, and I'm sure many a fine book has been written about them. It's just that they're not *my* concerns, so I pass those books by and move toward the ones that *do* address my interests. The truth is, I want to learn, but I want to learn about a limited number of issues. My learning will be within self-determined parameters. It is highly probable that I will never be much of an expert on physics, astronomy, archery, computers, or photography.

Which brings me to the next paradox pastors need to know: the Learning Paradox. This paradox says *you will only learn more of what you already know.* Even the most brilliant person in the world will not be interested in all of the books in the bookstore. We each find our own niche and do our learning there. Each of us is destined to become a master of something but not a master of everything.

The Learning Paradox has implications for the person who stands *in back of* the pulpit and for the people who sit *in front of* the pulpit. As a pastor, I need to know how the Learning Paradox affects me and also how it affects the people to whom I preach every Sunday.

Consider, first, how the paradox affects those of us who preach and serve as pastors. *We will only learn more of what we already know.* There is good news and bad news in that statement, and we need to know about both.

The good news is that limited knowledge can be concentrated knowledge, and that is not a bad thing. Acknowledging that we can only learn more of what we already know is, at least, an acknowledgment that we do know *something.* Focusing on that *something* can enable us to become specialists (dare I say experts?) on a particular issue. Specialists can often be more effective than generalists. Concentrating on a few things might serve us better over the long haul than dabbling in many things.

Is it really a bad thing that I will never become proficient at golf, hockey, or bowling because I have chosen to limit myself to playing tennis? Should I feel guilty that I will never master the flute, oboe, or saxophone because I have opted to learn the guitar? I think not, and I think I am better served to revel in the good news of the Learning Paradox: because I can't learn everything, I can decide to learn *a few things* well.

That truth touches my ministerial life too. I might not be particularly interested or gifted in certain tasks the church asks me to perform, but I *do* like to preach, and I *do* feel competent doing pastoral care. I might not be a biblical scholar in all parts of the canon, but I *do* know my way around the Sermon on the Mount, and I *do* have a decent grasp of the parables.

The Learning Paradox gives us permission to concentrate on our strengths and focus on the parts of our lives and ministries that most catch our fancy. It also prompts us to ponder an intriguing thought: ministerial proficiency might be more about strengthening strengths than improving weaknesses.

That's the good news of the Learning Paradox. It removes our guilt for being less than all-knowing, and it nudges us to follow our heart and our gifts.

But there is also a dark side to the Learning Paradox for those of us who pastor: because we can only learn more of what we already know, we can easily become one-dimensional people who never change. We can get stuck in a rut and spend our whole lives there.

I had a wise and wonderful uncle who was my mentor and confidant. One time I called him to vent my frustration about something and to wail about how I didn't seem to fit in the institutional church. He listened and, somewhere in the conversation, reminded me that I was "stuck with the way I was glued together."

He meant it as affirmation, and I took it that way. I have a certain temperament, a certain way of coming at life, and a certain theology that define me and keep me "glued together." But I also know that we can be "stuck with the way we are glued together" in a bad way. We can become inflexible, unchanging, no different at fifty than we were at twenty.

Is there anything sadder than a person who never changes?

Can you think of a worse ministerial fate that getting stuck in sameness, saying the same things over and over again, losing whatever spontaneity and originality we had? I have known pastors who have died on the vine, and it is not a pretty sight.

The dark side of the Learning Paradox reminds us of the necessity of thinking new thoughts, experimenting with new approaches, and establishing new relationships. We will never be masters of all things pastoral, but for God's sake (and our own and our congregation's), let's be masters of something. And let's endeavor to stay fresh and alive. Let's vow not to let the Learning Paradox doom us to a life of boring sameness.

That's the Learning Paradox from *in back of* the pulpit. That's how it impinges on us as pastors.

But think of it now as it impinges on those *in front of* the pulpit, those to whom we preach each week. Some of the people in front of the pulpit have "ears to hear." They are hungry for a word from the Lord. They lean forward in the pew. Sure, they have sung the songs a thousand times and heard the same text expounded many times as well, but they are happy to be at church. About them the Learning Paradox says, these people will only learn more of what they already know. They know the good news, and they are ready and willing to hear it again.

Like us, these people can become wooden, stale, and lifeless. Like us, they can put their minds on "automatic pilot" when they come to church. They can sing the songs, hear the word, and leave unchanged. But generally, these people do have "ears to hear." They want to be at church, and they sincerely want to hear a word from God.

I love these people, as do you. These are the people who teach the classes, serve on the committees, and, most importantly, pay our salaries! The church would have to close its doors if it were not for these fine people with "ears to hear" and hearts to respond.

But there are other people out there in front of the pulpit who *don't* have "ears to hear." These people find our whole worship service rather strange. The music is unfamiliar, the bread and juice bizarre, the baptism baffling, and the word about the cross unbelievable. These people fidget throughout the entire service, certain they are the only sane ones in a room of pious lunatics.

The Learning Paradox doesn't bring us good news about these people. If it's true that these people will only learn more of what they already know, our chances for reaching them are slim. This is not their world. This is not their fascination. These are not their songs. And this is not their gospel. The chances are good they will return to their own, familiar rut and resume digging there.

Occasionally, I see these people in the pews in front of me on Sunday morning. I know the teenager who comes only because her friends are there. I see the woman driven to church out of desperation because of her pending divorce. I notice the visitors who come because they're staying in the home of some of our church members. And I know about the grandparents who come because their granddaughter is singing in the children's choir.

They come and they go, untouched by what they see and hear. They simply don't have "ears to hear," and they can't become disciples of Jesus because he's not in their memory bank. What do we do about these people who show up at church deaf to our message and blind to our truth?

First, we entrust them to God. The Bible is full of stories about people who, against all odds, got "ears to hear." Think of the Twelve who dropped their jobs and routines and suddenly decided to follow Jesus. Or Paul, whose life took a dramatic turn while he was on a journey to Damascus. Or Zacchaeus, who invited Jesus over for dinner and ended up giving half of his possessions to the poor. Amazingly—no, *miraculously*—God still calls people who are not likely candidates for the kingdom, and from time to time they still say yes. We can be grateful that God has the power to override the negative implications of the Learning Paradox.

Second, we can try to understand them, not judge them. These people without "ears to hear" are not evil people, not any more evil than we are, really. They just don't know much about church things, haven't been exposed to biblical truth, and don't feel comfortable in our strange, religious environment. To throw stones at them or to assume a pious posture with them only serves to alienate them even more. My response, when I see them out there in the pews, should be to rejoice that they are there and to do everything in my power to make the gospel good news to them.

Third, we avoid the "language of Zion" as we teach and preach. I attended a financial seminar once and felt like a complete dimwit. The speaker was using terms he thought I understood, but I was completely lost. I didn't have the gumption to raise my hand and ask, "What exactly is a no-load fund?" We have our church jargon too, and this jargon can garble our message to newcomers. Most of them will never sidle up to us after to the service to ask, "What exactly *is* salvation?" They will just go away confused. Even if they came to church with "ears to hear," they will leave unchanged because they couldn't decipher our religious code.

Fourth, we celebrate when they change worlds. As I said, sometimes people get converted. They literally move from one world to another. Old things pass away; behold, all things become new. We can all think of people in our churches whose lives were radically altered by an encounter with God. When this happens, we should kill the fatted calf, throw a party, and make sure the decision is properly celebrated. It's a miracle, really. The Learning Paradox says that the likelihood of anyone changing worlds is slim indeed. But it happens, and when it does, it deserves a party.

The Learning Paradox leaves us with contradictory feelings regarding our listeners. It brings us joy when we think about those people with "ears to hear" but a distinct sadness when we think about those to whom our message is veiled. We can hope and pray, though, that even those who can't hear right now will someday be able to do so.

The next time you're in a bookstore, pay attention to what you do. Notice how you head only to those books about subjects that *already* fascinate you. Notice how you never go to the sections of the store that have books about new, unfamiliar topics. Just being aware of your bookstore shopping habits can remind you of the Learning Paradox: *You will only learn more of what you already know.*

Lest we get discouraged by this paradox and assume that both we and our listeners are destined for ruts and routine, I want to underscore the compensating truth that removes some of this paradox's sting: sometimes God trumps the Learning Paradox, and people get on a completely new road and move in a completely new direction. It still happens. Old things pass away. All things become new.

It still happens to weary preachers.

And it still happens to the people to whom we preach.

The Power Paradox

*The weakest people in the church
tend to wield the most power.*

Imagine two women who look to be almost clones of one another. Let's call them Paula and Pamela, and let's acknowledge that the casual observer would see them as twins, at least when it comes to their life situations.

Both Paula and Pamela are in their mid-forties and married with two teenaged children. Both are attractive, sophisticated college graduates. Both are Christians and belong to the same church. Coincidentally, both have just been elected by that church to serve on the personnel committee. It would seem, to the casual observer, that the committee inherited twins.

But closer scrutiny would reveal that these women actually have more differences than similarities. When the emotional and spiritual maturity of these women are considered, Paula and Pamela have little in common.

Paula, frankly, is a *pain*. Those who know her best are aware that Paula can wreak havoc on any group to which she belongs.

- Paula wants to change people into her image. She can't tolerate diversity and wants people to conform to her idea of rightness and respectability.
- Paula overreacts to the reactions of others. She plays a lot of emotional ping-pong, giving back to people exactly what she receives. If people are mad, she's mad. If people are unkind, she's unkind. She spends much of her time upset and emotionally distraught.
- Paula lacks a sense of humor and comes into any meeting deadly serious. To put it mildly, she is not known for her laughter and light-heartedness.
- Paula over-functions most of the time. She sees herself as someone who knows a lot and can do a lot, so she is not shy about asserting her authority. In the process, she often runs roughshod over others.
- Paula comes across as invulnerable. She is not influenced by either love or reason and shuts herself off from relational feedback.

- Paula talks *about* people instead of *to* them. She has been known to leave meetings and pick up the phone to tell church friends about "some of the awful things that are going on."
- Paula blames and judges others but sees herself as innocent. She is constantly mad and perpetually offended.

Paula is a disaster waiting to happen on any church committee on which she serves. But, of course, she gets asked nearly every year to be one of the leaders of the church.

Pamela, on the other hand, is a *prize*. Turn all of Paula's flaws rightside-up and you have sweet Pamela.

- Pamela has little interest in changing others. She knows she is far from perfect herself and has no desire to make others in her own image.
- Pamela is not particularly bothered by other people's emotions. If they get angry and rude, she has the capacity to stay unruffled and unbothered. She's not fond of emotional ping-pong.
- Pamela laughs a lot. The "emotional envelope" she brings to any committee is a light-hearted one that makes everyone breathe a little easier.
- Pamela will carry her weight on any committee, but she will not over-function or come across as bossy.
- Pamela is vulnerable and easily moved to both laughter and tears. She has an effective antenna and is receptive to the verbal and emotional feedback she receives.
- Pamela is not a gossip. She knows that talking *about* people is a sure way to sow discord in a group. When necessary, she does have the courage to talk *to* people about a problem.
- Pamela doesn't blame or judge others. She believes that "most people are doing the best they can with what they have to work with."

Here's the surprising and sad truth about these two women and their roles on the church personnel committee: troubled Paula will wield more power than sweet Pamela. The Power Paradox isn't one of the happier paradoxes of church life, but it is a true one: *The weakest people in the church tend to wield the most power.* Paula has more clout at church than Pamela.

Why is that? you might wonder. Why does a *pain* like Paula wield more power than a *prize* like Pamela? Are church people *that* blind to pains and prizes? Is there some subversive force at work in the church that makes people listen to Paula and ignore Pamela?

There is a subversive force at work here, but it is not confined to the church. This force infects all groups—families, corporations, schools, sports teams, and, yes, churches. The subversive force is what family systems theorists call "the leverage of the dependent." The weakest, most dependent members in any system end up with the most leverage and, therefore, the most power.

All we have to do to verify "the leverage of the dependent" is take an honest look around us. Look, for instance, at the family whose every move is dictated by an angry, troubled child. In accommodating to this child, the family grants her "the leverage of the dependent." The entire family does a dance around this troubled child so as not to upset her more, cause her more pain, or create a public scene. She, in effect, calls the shots and sets the agenda.

Look at the school classroom that is constantly interrupted by two or three disruptive students. These students set the agenda for the entire class. The teacher spends most of his time correcting these students or trying to placate them, and the learning rate for the class takes a nosedive. The class is governed by the bad behavior of a few students.

Look at the marriage in which one spouse has to tiptoe through life for fear of offending the other. Or the sports team that can't make a trade lest its superstar starts to sulk. Or the legislative body whose members are held hostage by a few wealthy donors back home. Or just about any other group trying to make progress and move forward into the future. Almost without fail, the recalcitrant minority thwarts the willing, progressive majority.

And this will certainly be true on that personnel committee at the church where Paula and Pamela serve. Paula will swing a bigger stick on that committee because she is a strong woman with a host of problems and because she knows people (especially church people) want harmony and consensus. When she threatens those two sacred cows, she can get almost anything she wants.

We sincerely want harmony at church. We would like to present to the world a community that is "one in the spirit, one in the Lord." We would sincerely like consensus, too. We would like to believe that God's Spirit is among us, leading us to the same conclusions about important matters. Because we so sincerely desire harmony and consensus, Paula has all of the leverage she needs to wield her power. She knows we will do almost anything to keep her happy lest she throw a hand grenade at our two sacred cows.

The pressing question for any pastor is this: How can I reverse the awful consequences of the Power Paradox? Left unchecked, this paradox will take the church straight to frustrating ineffectiveness. It means we will consistently accommodate the weakest people in our congregation to the detriment of everyone else. It means the church can never take up wings and fly like an eagle because it is always having to deal with a few surly turkeys who have no interest in flying.

I wouldn't profess for one moment to have the infallible answer to that pressing and practical question about the Power Paradox. I've seen my fair share of ecclesiastical turkeys through the years and moderated more than my share of business meetings where the reluctant minority sabotaged the progressive majority. I have the battle scars to prove the truth of the Power Paradox. But here are a few decisions I, as pastor to both Paula and Pamela, can make, decisions that might move our church more in the direction of health and progress:

First, I will not let Paula cause me undue grief. She is a woman who, in sweet Pamela's words, "is doing the best she can with what she has to work with." As her pastor, I will try to love her, minister to her, and nudge her along the Way. But I refuse to let her immaturity set *my* agenda. I will be self-differentiated enough to avoid playing her games. I won't get upset just because she is upset. I won't lose my sense of humor just because she has lost hers. And I won't let her petty "concerns about the church" become my concerns. In short, I won't lose much sleep over Paula.

Second, I will pay more attention to Pamela than Paula. If we aren't careful, we pastors can spend most of our days trying to "put out fires" started by immature people. We call people on the phone to soothe hurt feelings. We set meetings to arbitrate disputes. We spend our entire ministerial lives accommodating to weakness, and, of course, eventually get run down and burned out. But we can decide, instead, to pay attention to Pamela, to be around people who want good things to happen, to focus on strength instead of weakness. We have only so many hours in a day. Why not spend them with the people who can make positive things happen at church? We can decide to concentrate on the mature people in our church, not the immature.

Third, I will confront Paula if her attitude becomes a virus that affects the health of the church. In chapter 14, you'll read about the Confrontation Paradox. That paradox says that direct confrontation seldom confronts the problem. I truly believe that confronting people is usually a waste of time and energy and that it typically produces defensiveness and resistance. There are times, however, when Paula must be confronted. Even if the confrontation doesn't work and Paula becomes more resistant to change, it must be attempted. I can't stand idly by when Paula's venom starts making other people sick.

Fourth, I will keep in mind that there are worse tragedies than telling Paula good-bye. It is possible that Paula and her family might decide they can no longer be a part of our church. If church people refuse to cater to Paula's whims, if I as a pastor stand up to her attacks, and if she finally concludes she is not going to get her way, Paula might well conclude the Lord is calling her elsewhere. And certainly the Lord might be. My experience has been that when upset people leave a church, everyone benefits. The offended people might find a new church home where they fit better and can start anew. The church they leave behind breathes a silent sigh of relief they're gone. Truth to tell, no one on the personnel committee is too upset that Paula will no longer be tossing hand grenades into their meetings.

Fifth, I will remember that Pamela really is sweet and tell her so. Looking back on my thirty years as a pastor, I realize one obvious reality: the Pamelas have far outnumbered the Paulas in my ministry. I've had a few Paulas to contend with, but the overwhelming majority of people in my churches has been like Pamela. They've been kind, emotionally mature people who genuinely want the church to be the loving body of Christ. They've loved us, laughed with us, cooked for us, and made us know that our lives are encircled by people who care. And they've allowed me to be a weird, paradoxical pastor and embraced my quiet kind of leadership.

That's probably as good a way as any to end this chapter on an upbeat note, with the happy realization that in spite of the Power Paradox, these good, kind folks have somehow prevailed.

The Issues Paradox

The issues you most want to push
are beyond pushing.

Churches in the modern age troll for pastors who know how to grow a church. They are desperate for men and women who know how to promote, market, and sell. When the pulpit becomes empty, churches now look for sales-types, the same kinds of people who would succeed in real estate and life insurance.

That's why the old words of Karl Barth ought to be required reading for both pastors and pastor search committees:

> The word of God is not for sale; and therefore it has no need of shrewd sales-men. The word of God is not seeking patrons; therefore it refuses price cutting and bargaining; therefore it has no need of middlemen. The word of God does not compete with other commodities which are being offered to men on the bargain counter of life. It does not care to be sold at any price. It only desires to be its own genuine self, without being compelled to suffer alterations and mod-ifications. It will, however, not stoop to overcome resistance with bargain counter methods. Promoters' successes are sham victories; their crowded churches and the breathlessness of their audiences have nothing in common with the word of God.[1]

In spite of Barth's warning, the modern church has bought into the notion of the pastor as manager/salesperson/psychologist. And would-be pastors trolling for pulpits know what the market demands: "Seminary students are not blind to the fact that the big churches and the big salaries often go to those who are untheo-logical and even anti-theological. They know what kind of training they need: they need to become managers who have the status of professionals, not scholars, thinkers, or theologians."[2]

But this trend toward turning pastors into ecclesiastical corporate executives is destined to water down the true purpose of the church and lead people to the false notion that churches exist solely to get larger and richer. This trend is also destined to frustrate men and women who feel called of God to be *pastors*. Not salespeople. Not executives. Not fund-raisers. But *pastors*.

Just beneath this infatuation with results, numbers, and growth, just beneath the idea that pastors exist to *be dynamic and make things happen*, lies a falsehood that needs to be explored. The falsehood is that pastors have the power to *make things happen*. Oh, I suppose we pastors can make some things happen. We can raise money, comfort the bereaved, lead building campaigns, officiate at weddings and funerals, and play shortstop for the church softball team. We can do these things and more, but the things that truly matter—eternally matter—are beyond our power.

I think of the old cliché that says, "You can lead a horse to water, but you can't make it drink." That would be a fine saying to put on a plaque in every pastor's study. It would keep us tethered to the truth and do wonders for our attitude. We pastors can lead a horse to water. We have the power and know-how to do that. But we can't make that horse drink. We simply don't have the power or expertise to *make that happen*.

The next paradox we need to know about, then, is the Issues Paradox: *The issues you most want to push are beyond pushing.* What we'd like to see happen in people's lives—experiences like commitment, community, and celebration—are beyond our power. We simply can't push anyone into commitment, community, or celebration, and that truth has been known to frustrate many a preacher. The Issues Paradox brings us face to face with our limitations.

Think, for a moment, about those three desires.

We'd like the people who come to our church to find *commitment*. We want them to commit themselves to God. We want them to commit themselves to their spouses and children. We want them to commit themselves to a life of health and wholeness. We want them to take Jesus seriously and to commit themselves to following him.

We'd like the people who come to our church to find *community*. We want them to bear one another's burdens, laugh with one another, and know they are in a place where they can love and be loved. We desire for them close Christian friends and people who know them deeply.

And we'd like the people who come to our church to find *celebration*. We'd like them to understand that joy is the most infallible proof of the presence of God. We'd like them to see the church as an oasis in the desert, as the one place on earth where they can let loose and be glad.

Those are three wonderful wishes, and my guess is that most of us who are pastors wish them for our parishioners. But we also learn, early on, that we don't always get what we wish for. Even worse, we learn that it isn't appointed unto pastors to push those realities on church members or to create those realities for anyone. When it comes to commitment, community, and celebration, we can lead a horse to water, but we can't make it drink.

I think about all the people I've known through the years who have needed *commitment* in their lives. It was so obvious to me that they needed commitment to Jesus. And they needed to be in some committed relationships. And they needed to be committed to their jobs. They were adrift, with no real purpose or passion, nothing to anchor their days.

So I preached eloquent sermons about commitment to these folks. I told them about Jesus and the Sermon on the Mount and how building your life on his teachings was like putting your life-house on a rock foundation. I tried my best to model a life of commitment before them—loving Jesus myself, being faithful to my wife and children, and staying at the same church for twenty years.

But though I preached commitment to them and modeled commitment for them, some of these un-anchored souls never paid much attention. They seemed quite content with a life-house on sand, flimsy relationships, and bouncing from job to job. They heard my brilliant sermons, glanced at my exemplary life, and went on their merry way.

Is there anything more frustrating than that for a pastor? We know how crucial commitment is to abundant life. We know that without it people are destined for hard times. But commitment is a gift we can't bestow on others. It rises, like all of the truly significant things, from *within* a person. It can't be pushed on someone from outside.

Community is the same way. Haven't we all had experiences in which church fellowships, billed as fun, friendship-building events, flopped and made everyone miserable? Haven't we all seen people sitting glumly across from one another at Wednesday night suppers? Haven't we found ourselves stuck in social gatherings touted as fun and festive that are actually draining and depressing?

Community can't be pushed. We can create occasions where it can bloom, but that blooming is well beyond our control. *Forced intimacy* doesn't work and is really no intimacy at all.

Years ago, our church had a spiritual renewal weekend complete with leaders who came from out of town. One of the leaders informed me, when he arrived at our church, that the grand finale of the weekend would be a time at the end of the Sunday morning service when people filed by to tell Sherry and me how much they loved us. We were to stand at the front of the sanctuary while people, on command from the leader, filed by to express their love.

I told him we'd pass on that part of the weekend's agenda. He insisted that it would be a meaningful time for the church and for Sherry and me, but I was adamant. We didn't have the grand finale that weekend.

I was adamant about that because appreciation-on-command isn't appreciation at all. Just as community-on-command isn't community at all. If people, of their own volition, want to tell me they love me, I'll be grateful and thrilled. But if people tell me they love me because they've been told to do so, because it's part of a renewal weekend agenda, I want no part of it.

Yes, I want to be loved and appreciated. Yes, it's wonderful to try to build community. But community depends primarily on the inner workings of people and the chemistry that exists between them, not on techniques conjured by a "community builder." Like commitment, community must come from *within* people.

So, too, must *celebration*. Celebration can't be forced on anyone. When it comes to people being joyful and glad, you can't force that horse to drink.

I once heard about a church that wanted to do something creative in worship. On a particular Sunday, all of the worshipers were handed balloons as they came into the worship service. Then the pastor told the worshipers that worship is supposed to be a time of celebration and that the balloons were a reminder of the good news Christians have. He also told them that the good news is not be hoarded, but shared, that the joy they've found in Christ is to be released to the world. So, he said, when you feel especially celebrative this morning, when God really gets hold of you, release your balloon and let it soar to the ceiling.

It sounded like a creative, celebrative worship experience, but it went over like . . . well, like a lead balloon. At the end of the service, more than half of the worshipers still clutched their balloons, still waiting for God to get hold of them. I can almost picture the embarrassing scene at the end of that creative worship service: somber worshipers filing out of the sanctuary wondering what in the world they should do with this silly balloon. And dejected church staff people standing in the foyer collecting balloons and vowing never, ever to try another creative worship experience.

Is it the church's fault that those people can't feel glad enough to release their balloons? Maybe. Maybe the church's worship service *is* drab and joyless. Maybe the church is a lifeless place with lifeless worship. But I doubt it. My guess is that those people hanging on to their balloons don't have it in them to celebrate at church. The problem, I would guess, is with the people, not the worship service. A truly celebrative person would probably unleash the balloon at the first peal of the organ for the processional hymn. But a truly un-celebrative person couldn't hoist the balloon if Jesus himself walked into the sanctuary.

Like commitment and community, celebration is an inner phenomenon. We can decorate our sanctuaries with bright colors, play and sing upbeat music, preach the gospel with fervor, and be as friendly as any church on earth and still not stir celebration in the hearts of some people.

Shall we pastors call ourselves powerless, then, and seek a career in real estate? If we can't conjure commitment, community, and celebration in people, why are we wasting our time at church? Why not get an easier job that pays better? Shouldn't the Issues Paradox send us pastors scurrying to the woods in utter frustration? If we can't push what we really want to push, aren't we destined to a life of rolling the ball up the hill only to see it come tumbling down again?

Not really. I've come to see the Issues Paradox as good news for me as a pastor. I see it as good news for two reasons:

First, it reminds me that I'm not God. I can't invade other people's lives and inject them with commitment, community, and celebration. But God can. My role is to relax, be as real as I can be, do the best job I can do at church, and trust God to work in people's lives. What a relief it is to get off the throne of the universe! True, some people will never find commitment. Some will never live in a loving community. And some will never have a song in their hearts and celebrate life. But *I* can. Ultimately, I think that's what God expects of me.

Second, it restores to me the rightful role of the pastor. When I believe the pastor has the power to *make things happen*, I need to wear my manager/salesperson/psychologist uniform when I go to church. I need to push people to change and pull them into faith. It's all in my hands, and I'm responsible. Life becomes a strenuous tug-of-war, all in the name of God.

But once I recognize the Issues Paradox, I'm free to do the real work of the pastor: pray, preach, read, enjoy my calling, dream, rest, play, write. Those things might not *make things happen*, but then again they might. Those activities might not grow a huge institution or cause pastor search committees to start knocking down my door. But I'll be content, knowing I'm doing what I'm supposed to be doing and trusting that I'm not supposed to *make things happen* anyway.

God is.

[1] Quoted in David F. Wells, *God in the Wasteland* (Grand Rapids: Eerdmans, 1994), 60.

[2] David F. Wells, *No Place for Truth* (Grand Rapids: Eerdmans, 1993), 112-13.

The Decision Paradox

People seldom have to choose between right and wrong.

Once upon a time, not long ago it seems, I embarked on a journey to be a pastor. I felt call to do battle with the forces of evil in the name of God. I was going to be on the side of righteousness, of course, in a cosmic struggle with sin. Life was sharp in its distinctions in those early days—God/Satan, Light/Dark, Righteousness/Sin, Right/Wrong—and I was determined to be on the left side of those distinctions.

On top of that, I was going to help other people be on the left side of those distinctions as well. I was going to persuade people to choose God over Satan, light over dark, righteousness over sin, and right over wrong. I was going to hone my skills as a minister—preaching, counseling, witnessing, praying—so that I could be an effective ambassador for the left side.

At some indefinable point in my ministry, though, I discovered the Decision Paradox: *People seldom have to choose between right and wrong.* It completely exploded my early concept of ministry, but I do believe that knowing about this paradox has made me a wiser pastor and a better person.

Frankly, I'm surprised now I didn't learn the Decision Paradox earlier. I kept bumping into it, but my old training in seeing life as a series of either/or propositions blurred my vision. I began to notice, though, that people in my church did not have to make decisions between right and wrong. When they talked to me about the gut-wrenching issues they were dealing with, my old template of black and white was useless. Come to find out, these people were not wrestling with black and white decisions at all. They had to choose among various shades of gray.

• The family with the husband and father on life support. Should they keep him hooked up indefinitely, or should they pull the plug? How would they know when it was time to take him off the machine?

- The parents with their troubled teenager. Should they take him out of school and send him to a rehab boot camp facility? Or should they leave him alone and hope he comes to his senses and rights his course?
- The finance committee with its unexpected budget surplus. Should the committee, in an extravagant gesture of gratitude, propose that we give all of the surplus to a mission effort in India? Or should the committee recommend that we use the money to address pressing needs in our own church?
- The old couple living in their beloved house for fifty years. In light of their health problems, should they move to an assisted living facility? But then again, in light of their long history in that house, could they bear to leave it? Which way should they go?

I discovered these were the kinds of issues with which people struggled. Not one of these issues was black and white or cut and dried. Not one of them fit the ministerial template I had imposed upon reality. Not one of them needed a crusader on a white horse with simplistic answers. This was the real stuff of life, and it had nothing to do with choosing God over the devil. It had everything to do with trying to discern the will of God in a complicated, gray world.

Knowing and affirming the Decision Paradox has affected my life as a pastor in at least four ways:

First, it has enabled me to look at the "gray-ness" in my own life. You see, not only did I discover that the world is more complicated than simple blacks and whites; I also discovered that *I* am a mixed bag of blacks and whites. This paradox reigns not only in the world at large; it reigns in my own heart. I am more complicated and "gray" than I care to say.

My old image of myself as the "good pastor" with the "good answers" trying to convince bad people to become "good people" went down in a heap of honest reality. The truth, I discovered as I wrestled with the real issues real people brought to me, is that I am a confused sinner myself, not some pristine, lily-white answer-man for God.

For one thing, I'm not a "good pastor." I am a pastor, for sure, but one with his own problems and "issues." To call myself "good" is more than a stretch.

I am not loaded with "good answers" either. I think I have learned a few things along the way, but I know a lot less now than I did when I was crusading atop my white horse. I no longer think I have to dispense simple answers to people's complicated problems.

And, for that matter, I no longer think I need to convince bad people to become "good people." It has turned out that some of those bad people are better people than me, even more Christian than me. I no longer say or imply, "Come, be as good as me," but "Let's all go throw our floundering selves on the mercy of God."

It's a painful thing for pastors to have to come to grips with their own humanity, their own invisible web of mixed motives and tangled flaws. In a passage from Robertson Davies' novel *Fifth Business*, a woman named Liesl chides an uptight Calvinist named Ramsey for not admitting his humanity:

> You should take a look at this side of your life you have not lived. Now don't wriggle and snuffle and try to protest. I don't mean you should have secret drunken weeks and a widow in a lacy flat who expects you every Thursday, like some suburban ruffian. You are a lot more than that. But every man has a devil, and a man of unusual quality, like yourself, Ramsey, has an unusual devil. You must get to know your personal devil. You must even get to know his father, the Old Devil. Oh, this Christianity! Even when people swear they don't believe in it, the fifteen hundred years of Christianity that has made our world is in their bones and they want to show they can be Christians without Christ. Those are the worst; they have the cruelty of doctrine without the poetic grace of myth.[1]

I'm trying to come to grips with my own devil. And I've learned that I can't be a Christian without Christ.

Second, it has enabled me to sit more comfortably in the silence. Without an awareness of the Decision Paradox, I felt obligated to provide airtight answers to people. When they grieved, I had to tell them why God had taken their loved one. When they came with perplexing questions about the Bible, I had to give them an impressive response. When they were angry with God, I had to defend God and quote Scriptures to back up my defense. Without the Decision Paradox, I had to be an answer-man, a holy encyclopedia of retorts and responses.

But once I learned the Decision Paradox, I gave that up. I don't have to tell anyone why God took their loved one. I don't know why that person died, so why pretend? I don't have to have every answer to every question about the Bible. Some of the Bible is so mystifying I have no clue how to interpret it. And when someone is angry with God, I usually think that person has every right to be angry, and I make little effort to defend or protect God. I might even sit beside that person in her grief and rail at God myself.

Since most of the decisions people have to grapple with are various shades of gray, why try to inject black and white into the mix? Why not sit with them in silence in the grayness of it all, seeking the will of God, asking not for answers but for Presence?

Understanding the Decision Paradox, that people seldom have to choose between right and wrong, means that I'm free—no, *called*—to sit with people at the crossroads and not yell advice at them.

Third, it has kept me from being seduced by the false dichotomies of our culture. Because the Decision Paradox makes me aware of nuance and subtlety, it rescues me from the "broad brush" mentality used in television and newspapers. The media must communicate in sound bites and headlines, which means there is no place at all for nuance and subtlety.

According to the media, you have to be pro-homosexuality or anti-homosexuality, pro-abortion or anti-abortion, pro-president or anti-president, Republican or Democrat, conservative or liberal. Because time and space are short, the media must paint with a broad brush, and we all get the idea that reality is an either/or experience. We're either in this camp, or we're in the opposing camp. Life on screen and page is depicted as cut and dried.

But, as I said, life in the real world is anything *but* cut and dried. Not all homosexuals are exactly alike. Not all abortions are exactly alike either. It is possible to like some things about the president and despise other things. It is also possible to vote Republican one election and Democrat the next election and to be conservative on some issues and liberal on others. Life in the real world is messy, gray, and complicated and can't be captured in sound bites and headlines.

As a pastor aware of the Decision Paradox, I can admit that fact and minister accordingly. I can take up residence in the uncomfortable "middle" and not identify with any of the extremes the media portrays. I know that life is not really black and white and that many of the decisions people have to make are not black and white either.

Truthfully, I don't care much about people's politics, social stands, or voting records. I'm called to minister to people regardless of their ideology. Some of the people in my church are tree-huggers and feminists. Some listen to Limbaugh every day. Some are theological liberals who read Spong, and some are conservatives who read Dobson. But I'm called to be the pastor of all these folks, and I'm not going to let a label get in the way.

I've learned that all of them—liberals and conservatives, Christians and non-Christians, Republicans and Democrats—have to make tough decisions that are seldom black and white. If I can provide them some wisdom in that process or be a pastoral presence of love in that process, I will be giving them the best gift I can offer.

Fourth, it has informed my preaching and invited me to be honest in the pulpit. When I remember that life is not usually black and white and that the decisions people have to make are not black and white, I can then try to fashion sermons that better match the real colors of their world.

I realize now that for years my sermons have been a whole lot simpler than reality is. For years, I have handed searching people three points and a poem. More than I care to admit, my sermons are still simpler than real life.

But knowing the Decision Paradox at least helps me try to craft sermons that match people's experience of life. If the decisions they are wrestling with are tough, gray, and complicated, I can hardly justify sermons that are easy, white, and simple. If I give them enough of those easy, white, simple sermons, they will eventually shake my hand at the door on Sunday morning and tell me how wonderful the message was, but then they'll leave knowing that I don't really have a clue.

I have kept all of my sermon notes through the years. I have dozens of folders bulging with homiletical masterpieces. Sometimes when I'm feeling especially courageous, I flip through those folders and look at some of the trivia I've foisted off on good people. I see sermons on how to be happy, how to know the will of God, how to hear the voice of God, how to survive a tragedy, how to raise happy children. When I peruse those folders I see that I've been heavy on the "how to's."

I've also been heavy on the easy, white, and simple. Some of those sermons have three or four points, the first word often beginning with the same letter. If only the "four C's" could really connect a person to God. If only the "3 P's" could guarantee parents happy children. But life simply won't conform to the structure of those old sermons, and the most appropriate place for them is probably the dumpster out behind the fellowship hall.

But I'm getting better. The older I get, the more honest I become. And the older I get, the more I try to craft sermons in the image of life itself. The Decision Paradox has nudged me toward authenticity.

There are still days when I grow wistful for how it used to be. I long for the days of certainty, days when I saw myself on the white horse rushing to the rescue of people looking for black and white answers. On busy weeks, when I lack sufficient time to prepare a sermon, I occasionally take out one of those old sermons, brush the dust off of it, and give it a go.

Inevitably, the sermon fizzles. I know better now, and my heart is not in "The Six Ways to Know the Will of God." I know that life is not as simple as my sermon and that to reach modern people, I had better get in touch with their experience.

Among other things, I have the Decision Paradox to thank for that.

[1] Robertson Davies, *Fifth Business* (New York: Penguin, 1970), 226.

The Influence Paradox

The most powerful people in your
life will not be powerful people.

If I were to ask you to name a powerful person, who comes to mind?

You might think of someone with physical power, like a defensive lineman in the NFL or your next-door neighbor who "pumps iron" for hours every day. If your goal is to move furniture, demolish a wall, or sack a quarterback, those are exactly the kinds of people you need.

You might think of someone with political power, like the president of the United States or the mayor of your city. If you need to pass important legislation, those people have the necessary power to get it done.

You might think of someone with financial power—a Bill Gates, Donald Trump, or Warren Buffett who has more money than he can spend in a lifetime. If you need to underwrite an expensive business endeavor, those are the kinds of people with sufficient funds to make it happen.

But what if the task at hand doesn't require physical, political, or financial power? What if you want to teach a child to read? What if you need to repair a broken marriage? What if you want to compose a song? What if you want to reconcile with your rebellious teenage son? To accomplish those things, physical, political, or financial power would do you no good. You would need a different kind of power.

Years ago, I read a definition of power that has been helpful to me ever since: "Power is the ability to accomplish purpose." That is a helpful definition because it reminds us that power is more than might or force.

If I showed you an ax that weighs ten pounds and a razor that weighs a few ounces and asked you which was the most powerful tool, what would you say? Well, the correct answer depends on your purpose. If you need to chop down a tree, the ax has the most power. But if you need to get a close shave, the razor is actually the more powerful tool. It has the ability to accomplish that purpose.

Martin Luther drew a distinction between what he called "right-handed power" and "left-handed power." Right-handed power is direct, confrontational, and noticeable. It is the defensive lineman sacking a quarterback, the president vetoing a bill, or Trump buying a shopping mall. When we think of power, we usually have in mind the right-handed variety.

But there is also left-handed power. This power is indirect, non-confrontational, and often unnoticed. Left-handed power is a mother taking care of her disabled child, a kindergarten teacher teaching her class the alphabet, or a father enduring the pain of a prodigal son. Left-handed power has the strange look of non-intervention.

As Robert Capon puts it in his book, *Parables of the Kingdom*:

Left-handed power is paradoxical power. It looks for all the world like weakness. It is the intervention that seems indistinguishable from non-intervention. More than that, there is no guarantee that it will stop determined evildoers, though it might, of course, touch and soften their hearts. But then again, it might not. It certainly didn't for Jesus. And if you decide to use it, you should be quite clear that it probably won't for you either. The only thing it does insure is that you will not—even after your chin has been bashed in—have made the mistake of closing any interpersonal doors from your side.[1]

That hardly seems like power, does it? But it *is* power, so much power that evil can't touch it. Left-handed power is God's kind of power, the power of the cross, the power of forgiveness. And the gates of hell cannot prevail against it.

I'm telling you this about the two kinds of power so that I can angle toward our next paradox. I can make this paradox clearer, I think, if you have the notion of left-handed power in your mind.

The Influence Paradox says that *the most powerful people in your life will not be powerful people.* Another way of saying that would be "the most powerful people in your life will be the ones with left-handed power." They will not be powerful people in the sense that they have a lot of physical strength, political clout, or large sums of money; they will be powerful people in the sense that they refuse to coerce you, they love you in spite of yourself, and they give you every opportunity to spurn their love and "bash their chin in."

Influence is all about left-handed power. All we have to do to verify that is think about the most influential people in our lives. The most powerful people in our lives are not the ones who have forced us into anything or pressured us into subservience. They are the ones who have invited us into a relationship of love and then left the ball in our court.

When we think about what our relationships need most, inevitably we realize that they rise and fall with the paradoxical power of the left hand, not the direct, confrontational power of the right.

Take marriage, for instance. What does a wife need from her husband? Does she need him to be more authoritative, boss her more, push her into submission? Or does she need him to be more open, vulnerable, and loving and then trust her to respond? What does a husband need from his wife? That she henpeck him into change? That she browbeat him with good advice? Or that she be patient, accepting, and kind?

For that matter, what do our children need? And our parents? And our coworkers? What does the *world* need, really? My guess is we all need to give and receive some left-handed power, to quit trying to be in charge of one another, to lay down our "to-do" lists for one another, and to try, for a change, the power of the cross. What the world needs now is not just love, sweet love, but the awesome power of the left hand.

Once we're acquainted with left-handed power, we have no trouble grasping the Influence Paradox. We know that the people who will be most powerful and influential are not the ones our world has deemed powerful and influential, but the mostly unnoticed people who touch others with quiet love.

Knowing about this paradox reminds those of us who are pastors that our best and finest ministry will go undetected by the masses. The most Christlike things we do will receive no acclaim. Our best and truest acts as pastors will never make headlines. They will be accomplished by a certain look from our eyes, the sound of our voice, or something we write in a letter to a friend. I'm now convinced that my most lasting ministry has nothing to do with sermons to big crowds or church growth statistics. When it comes to lasting ministry, I know I'm playing to a very small crowd.

Maybe a personal experience from the world of sports will make my point more clearly. When my son Randel was playing high school football, I was rather ambivalent about the head coach. He wasn't particularly friendly, and his personality wouldn't win any prizes. Since Randel was a wide receiver, I firmly believed we needed to install a pass-oriented offense. Our coach was a strong believer in running the football, though, and we didn't throw the ball nearly as much as I would have liked. The coach obviously didn't know what a potential star he had in the Edwards kid.

But our team roared through the regular season, losing only one game and running up gaudy statistics. We even threw the ball enough to get the Edwards kid some mention in local newspapers. He got to catch passes and score a handful of touchdowns.

When we entered the play-offs, the scores got closer, but we still won our first two games easily. The third play-off game was a different story. It was a nail-biter, and with just a few minutes left in the game we were behind by four points but driving for the go-ahead touchdown. It was then that our coach "wised up" and decided to go to his ace wide receiver. Our quarterback threw a low, off-target pass to Randel, but he made a spectacular diving catch, and the drive continued.

But wait. The referee was making a strange motion as if there had been a fumble on the play and the other team had recovered. None of us in the stands saw what had happened, but we did see the official definitely signal that the other team now had the ball. Well, our chances for victory went down the drain on that play. Randel walked dejectedly to the sideline. Sherry, Stacy, and I sat in stunned silence in the stands. We were heartbroken for the ace wide receiver.

What happened next was surprising and amazing. You have to understand that when I was playing high school football, our coach was an angry man who spewed venom on us whenever we made a mistake. We lived in fear of fumbles, lest we incur the wrath of Coach Garrison. So I expected the same treatment for my son. I assumed the coach would berate him for such a costly fumble in such a big game.

But he didn't. Instead, I saw him put his arm around Randel's shoulders and say something quietly in his ear. Then he patted him on the back. He wasn't berating him; he was consoling him. He was trying to make him feel better, not worse, about the fumble.

That happened ten years ago, but I remember it like it happened yesterday. I don't remember much else about our coach, really. I can't recall the scores of the games anymore, and my son's statistics have even faded a bit in my memory. But I *do* remember the sermon about forgiveness the coached preached at the end of that play-off game. I doubt that anyone else in the stands even noticed his gesture of kindness, but I noticed it, and it moves me still when I think about it.

I remember Randel's coach not for his win/loss record, his stirring pre-game speeches, or his fabulous personality. I remember him for slipping his arm around my son's shoulders and teaching him the meaning of the word "grace."

That—or something like that—is what I'm talking about when I say a pastor's best ministry will go undetected by the masses. The most powerful, influential acts we do will be small, left-handed acts, like putting our arm around a shoulder, laughing in the face of pressure, or being silly with a child.

Richard Farson, in *Management of the Absurd*, told of an informal survey he once conducted with a number of adults about their childhoods. He asked them the question, "As you think back over your childhood and the relationship you had with your parents, can you remember any specific actions or events that you particularly value and that seem to you to have been significant in your development?"

Their answers were both surprising and instructive:

- My parents had make-believe fights with wet dishcloths.
- When I sat on my dad's lap, he pretended to scold me because my hair tickled his chin.
- We loved it when Mom made believe she was Dracula and scared us.
- My father, in his coat and tie, sat on the ground with me and ate these dirty baked potatoes I had cooked in the backyard.
- When I was learning to drive, I ran into the same car three times, but Mom took the blame.
- We really liked it when our parents did their silly monster walk in the supermarket.[2]

When I think about my own parents, my best memories are of similar things: Mom doing "the jitterbug" with her sisters, Dad guessing which baseball star I was mimicking as I assumed a variety of batting stances in the living room. I remember them best and love them most for little, seemingly insignificant things that made them real and human.

That's what the Influence Paradox is all about: *The most powerful people in your life will not be powerful people.* And the most memorable moments you will ever have might not be memorable to anyone but you.

The Influence Paradox has many implications for me as a pastor but none more pointed than the one I've mentioned: My most significant ministry will not be seen as impressive, formal ministry at all. My most significant ministry will take place in small, left-handed ways that have nothing to do with building an institution or delivering spellbinding sermons. When they write my obituary, they might tell of all the years I was at a church, how large the church became under my leadership, or how many buildings were built during my pastorate. But that's not the measure of my true effectiveness.

I will consider myself "successful" as a pastor if a few people remember the touch of my hand on their shoulder, a touch that communicated more eloquently than words the meaning of grace.

[1] Robert Capon, *Parables of the Kingdom* (Grand Rapids: Zondervan, 1985), 23.

[2] Richard Farson, *Management of the Absurd* (New York: Simon & Schuster, 1996), 32.

The Controversy Paradox

The issue you are arguing about is not the issue at all.

Once, my friend was having such serious pain in her neck that she was miserable for weeks. She couldn't sleep at night, walk with her normal posture, or even laugh without feeling pain. She sought out one doctor after another but to no avail. These doctors prescribed treatments and medicine for her aching neck, but nothing helped.

Then she heard about a female therapist in Austin. This therapist was not a doctor, as such, but an expert in manipulating and massaging the body to find and alleviate pockets of pain. My friend made an appointment with this therapist and was amazed at what happened when she went to see her.

The therapist began to probe for the cause of her neck pain, but she didn't limit her examination to the neck. She massaged and manipulated different parts of her body and eventually found the source of her pain. It was in her left foot! The therapist pushed hard at a certain pressure point on the underside of my friend's foot, and the pain in her neck subsided immediately. My friend was able to leave the therapist's office with her head held high because, for the first time in months, her neck pain was gone.

Who would have guessed that the cause of her neck pain was a problem in her foot? Only a paradoxical kind of therapist would have tried treating a foot to remedy a sore neck.

When my friend's husband told me of her experience at the therapist's office, I found a perfect illustration of a phenomenon I've seen over and over in the church. It's the Controversy Paradox: *The issue you are arguing about is not the issue at all.* Unless we know about this paradox, we will logically assume that a neck problem in the church originates in the neck, when we should be paradoxically assuming that it might originate in the foot.

For example:

- The woman who is constantly badgering us about our office hours (or lack thereof!) actually has a problem with her father that traces all the way back to her childhood. We could be in our office ten hours every day and not quell her criticism. The issue of office hours is not really the issue.
- The man who consistently complains about our lack of attention to his relatives in the hospital actually want us to pay attention to *him. He* feels neglected and inferior and desperately yearns for pastoral attention. We can visit every one of his relatives in every hospital in town and not touch the real problem. The issue of his relatives being neglected is not really the issue.
- The anger at the pastor from certain people in the church actually dates back twenty years when a pastor embezzled money from the church. Resentment got in the system twenty years ago and has never gotten out of the system. Any pastor at that church will face a pocket of resistance from those with long memories—and even from people who weren't around when the pastor embezzled the money but have inherited the anger and anxiety from those who were. The most perfect pastor in the world is destined for headache and heartache at this church because the current pastor's behavior is not really the issue.
- The staff member who can't get along with the rest of the staff actually has a problem with his wife. Every day he hauls his marital frustration to the church, and it spills over into his relationships with his coworkers. The other staff members have tried hard to get along with him and feel guilty that their efforts have gone for naught. But the truth is, they can do everything relationally right and still not help the situation. The issue of staff relations is not really the issue.

I could go on, but you get the point. In the church, it is almost a given that any time you have a neck ache, you'd better check your foot first! *The issue you are arguing about is not the issue at all.*

Friedman, in *Generation to Generation,* wrote:

> Whether the particular issue is criticism of clergy functioning, a problem related to administration, adequate salary, a sabbatical, or a theological matter, when such issues subtly surface, and with great intensity, or when they won't go away despite numerous, reasonable efforts to compromise with the more vociferous, then the issues under dispute are not the issues.[1]

Since this paradox raises its head so frequently in church life, what are some of the implications for those of us who serve in church leadership positions? More to the point, how does knowing about the Controversy Paradox help us?

First, it enables us to be less defensive when we feel under attack. Friedman went on to say, "Much of the criticism directed at spiritual leaders is henpecking, pure and simple. It can never be made to go away permanently by trying harder to please. Despite the time-bomb quality of the emotionality, it is usually rather harmless in itself and will tend to self-destruct if there is no defensive feedback to keep it ticking."[2]

Two ideas in that paragraph deserve elaboration. The first is that much of the criticism we have to put up with *is* henpecking. This criticism is also displaced anxiety from families of origin, poor marriages, and past experiences with church leaders. In other words, much criticism has little to do with us and needs to be received in that light. When it comes to "the problem with the pastor," the issue is usually not the issue.

The second thing worth mentioning in Friedman's paragraph is the part about the criticism being rather harmless in itself and that it will self-destruct if there is no defensive feedback to keep it ticking. That means we only exacerbate the problem by defending ourselves. The more emotional and vociferous we get in proclaiming our innocence, the more feedback we provide to keep the criticism alive. This dovetails nicely with the Anxiety Paradox, which we looked at earlier: *The less you worry about the church, the better it will do.* When it comes to criticism, the less uptight we are about it and the less we try to vindicate ourselves, the better we will do.

Does that mean we should be meek lambs, never standing up for ourselves? Not at all. If someone levels a serious charge against us, we should refute it vigorously. But when the criticism is of the henpecking variety—the petty, inconsequential gripes about pastoral performance that are part and parcel of being a pastor we do well to pay them little heed. Defending ourselves against henpecking just energizes the process and keeps the criticism going.

I read once about a priest in a small town who was being criticized by his parishioners. The criticism finally escalated to the point that certain members of the church drew up a petition enumerating the priest's faults and demanding his resignation. When the priest found out that the petition was being circulated throughout the parish, he tracked it down, and then signed it himself!

Second, it will keep us from dealing with problems that don't exist. If the Controversy Paradox is true and the issue we're arguing about is not really the issue, we're wasting our time to continue arguing about it. Think about the situations I mentioned earlier. If we ignore the Controversy Paradox, we will:

- spend countless hours in the office at church trying to show our resident critic that we really are responsible. But it won't help. Until she makes peace with her father, until she takes care of her family-of-origin issues, the criticism will not subside. Or, if it does, it will just resurface in another "problem."
- run ourselves ragged trying to get around to see all of the man's relatives in all of the hospitals in town. But again, our diligence won't touch the real issue. Until we show the man himself some attention, until we deal directly with him and his inferiority complex, we're wasting our time and gasoline running all over town to see his kin.
- worry ourselves sick over the irrational anger of some people in our church. We can't seem to win their approval, no matter how hard we try, and it drives us crazy. But if the real issue is what happened with the former pastor twenty years ago, we're going crazy in vain. Until those old wounds are addressed and dealt with, the anger toward the pastor will never go away.
- fret over how to get along with the surly staff member and feel guilty that we don't feel close to him. But if the real issue is his marriage and his frustrating relationship with his wife, we're spinning our wheels with our fretting and guilt. It would be wiser to quit catering to his obnoxious behavior and get the church to pay for marriage counseling for him.

It's foolish to keep focusing on your neck if the real problem is your foot! The Controversy Paradox helps us search until we discover the pressure point that will alleviate the pain.

Finally, it helps us remember that a system gets unstuck by taking risks and seeking adventure, not by focusing on the problem. Without an awareness of the Controversy Paradox, we get in a cause-and-effect way of thinking in the church that prohibits real problem-solving. We try to locate the "problems" in the church so we can then come up with the "solutions."

We gather data, do surveys, study demographic information, look at what other churches are doing, read the latest books on church life, and spend months formulating long-range plans. Eventually, we have a mind-boggling amount of data and feel almost overwhelmed. We are faced with a true dilemma: Now that we have gathered all of this data, what are we going to do with it? And now that we have assessed our problem, can we find the perfect "solution"?

This cause-and-effect thinking doesn't match life in the real world. Life is not that simple. Certainly *church life* is not that simple. When our church is "stuck," cause-and-effect, the-issue-is-the-issue thinking will not get us moving:

. . . when any relationship system is imaginatively gridlocked, it cannot get free simply through more thinking about the problem. Conceptually stuck systems cannot become unstuck simply by trying harder. For a fundamental reorientation to occur, that spirit of adventure which optimizes serendipity and which enables new perceptions beyond the control of our thinking processes must happen first. This is equally true regarding families, institutions, whole nations, or entire civilizations.[3]

What that means for the church is that taking risks and seeking adventure are better medicine than taking surveys and seeking opinions. When the church has "problems" and "weaknesses," it's time to do something risky and adventuresome: build a house for Habitat, plan a big mission trip, start a soup kitchen for the homeless, reorganize the structural system of the church.

Don't focus on the "problems" and "weaknesses." Take risks and seek adventure, and the problems and weaknesses will go away.

It's interesting to remember how Jesus dealt with people like Zacchaeus and the rich, young ruler. They came to Jesus with problems and wanted answers. But Jesus didn't answer either of them. Instead, he invited both of them to take a risk and seek adventure. He invited them to get rid of their "stuff" and gamble their lives on him. If they would do that, Jesus must have known, their problems would take care of themselves.

That's just the way life works, and the Controversy Paradox reminds us of it. We don't fix the problem by directly addressing the problem; we fix the problem by doing something risky and adventuresome. That's true for the church. And it's also true for us as individuals.

---

[1] Edwin Friedman, *Generation to Generation* (New York: Guilford, 1985), 202-203.

[2] Ibid., 207.

[3] Edwin Friedman, *A Failure of Nerve* (Bethesda MD: Edwin Friedman Estate, 1999), 38.

The Confrontation Paradox

Direct confrontation seldom confronts the problem.

You know, of course, that everything in this book could be wrong. It all comes from my skewed thinking, warped personality, and peculiar experiences, and anything coming from that steamy cauldron of fallibility is destined to be less than perfect. So take it all with a grain of salt.

This next paradox, for example, could be just a function of my own dislike of conflict and confrontation. I hate conflict and avoid it like the plague—always have, always will.

I also don't respond well when someone confronts me. I have a serious stubborn streak that makes me defensive when directly criticized. If someone marches into my study today and confronts me with my deficiencies, it likely won't prompt me to repent. It will prompt me, instead, to withdraw from my confronter and stay even more stuck in my deficiencies. I wish it weren't so, but it is.

And my guess is that I'm not unique. I think most people are like that. So I offer you next the Confrontation Paradox: *Direct confrontation seldom confronts the problem.* In my experience, direct confrontation creates more problems than it solves.

Tom Peters, in *The Pursuit of WOW!*, agrees: "I don't think conflict makes much sense. Your scintillating personality and brilliant analytic skills rarely turn enemies into allies. And win or lose, you waste . . . a lot of time training for the battle and cleaning up the mess."[1]

Of course this flies in the face of the great wisdom in some of the best-selling books on leadership. We're told in those books that "strong leaders" regularly confront people about their mistakes and limitations, ask them to toe the line, and tell them to shape up or ship out. We get the idea that real leaders come in only one shape and size: the tough people who aren't afraid to yell, demand, and confront.

But if that's what it takes to be pastoral leader, count me out. I've found that with my skewed thinking, warped personality, and peculiar experiences, being that kind of leader is impossible. It seems to me that "confrontational leadership" builds walls, not bridges, and I want no part of it.

With the Confrontation Paradox as a key component in my personal approach to leadership, I've had to do leadership by different rules. When I try to write them down and put them in a coherent form, my nonconfrontational leadership plan looks something like this:

• *Confront only as a last resort.* Some people use confrontation as the first step in correcting a problem. They go where angels fear to tread and quickly take people to task for their mistakes. As I said, I think it is a foolish, destructive thing to do. Hear Tom Peters again: "Head-on fights are stupid. Well, that's not always the case: Sometimes they serve a symbolic end, showing people you're tough, or some such . . . . In general, though, they're to be avoided. Fighting drains an enormous amount of emotional energy and usually makes you look like a jerk."[2]

Are there times when confrontation is necessary? No doubt. If people are blatantly hurting themselves or others, they need to be confronted. But that is the last step, not the first one. It's the step we take only after all others have been tried. It's the step we take only when we'll concede to building walls and not bridges.

• *Make your relationships tender, not tough.* Some leaders pride themselves in being tough. They like tough love, tough talk, tough business, even tough Christianity. These are the leaders prone to quick anger and quick confrontation.

But I'm a firm believer that negotiation is a better leadership tool than confrontation. Negotiation asks, "Have you ever thought about doing it this way? Can I work with you to make this happen? What do you need to improve in this area? What can I do to make life better for you?" Negotiation is a softer, gentler way to come at people.

Confrontation communicates, "I have the answer from on high and need to set you straight." Negotiation communicates, "We're in this together and together we can get it done." Confrontation is one-sided and inhibits intimacy. Negotiation is two-sided and encourages intimacy. Confrontation is tough. Negotiation is tender.

• *Make Jesus your model for leadership, not General Patton, Coach Lombardi, or Genghis Khan.* As I mentioned at the beginning of this book, we are awash in a sea of books about leadership. These books invite leaders to learn from people

THE LEADERSHIP LABYRINTH

like George Patton, Vince Lombardi, and even Genghis Khan. Though I haven't read many of these books, they probably contain practical, useable truths.

But long ago another Book was written that invites us to make Jesus our leadership hero, and since that Book has unmistakable credibility, we pastors would do well to stick with it. The New Testament gives us Jesus as the consummate leader, and when we look to him for help with the confrontation issue, we discover that Jesus was tender, not tough. At least he was tender with most people.

The most glaring exception was the way Jesus confronted the religious leaders of his day. As you well remember, he directly confronted them with their false, hypocritical approach to God. I think, for example, of the "woes" in Matthew 23 and Luke 11 where Jesus scalds the Pharisees and rebukes them for their petty religion. In these passages, he minces no words and softens no blows, reminding us, I suppose, that sometimes confrontation *is* necessary.

Generally, though, Jesus wasn't a confronter. The "woe" passages are the exception, not the rule. The reason we remember the "woes" and an incident like the cleansing of the temple is because they seem so out of character for Jesus. He usually didn't resort to such direct, forceful confrontation.

Think of how he related to the outcasts and sinners. He typically didn't castigate them for their sins; he told them delightful stories that showed them a better way, and he invited them to become a part of a new kingdom. Think about the Sermon on the Mount, where he sketched a whole new approach to life without once condemning his listeners or twisting any arms. Think about him stooping to wash his disciples' feet, showing them once and for all that leadership is not about tyranny, but a towel. Think about him standing before Pilate, quietly in control, quietly refusing to get in a power game.

More to the point, think about Jesus in your own experience. Has he "bowled you over" and revealed himself to you in direct, obvious ways? Or has he come quietly to your heart's door and waited patiently for you to invite him in? Have you been confronted by a loud Jesus or wooed by a quiet Jesus?

I can only speak for myself, but he has come to me as a quiet presence, and frankly I sometimes get frustrated that he's not more wide-screen and Technicolor. He has in no way forced himself upon me. He has left my response to me, and if I take Jesus as my leadership role model, I will do the same for others. I will offer myself to them, not force myself upon them. Except on rare occasions, I will be in the "quiet" camp, not the "loud" camp.

• *Forget your detractors.* When you read the Gospels, you get the impression that Jesus was literally hounded by the religious leaders of his day. Try as he might, he couldn't escape them. But you also get the impression that they didn't set his agenda. He didn't plan his day around the antics of the scribes and Pharisees. He basically ignored them unless they became such a nuisance that he had to address them. Truthfully, he didn't go out of his way to confront them. They confronted him, and he spoke in rebuttal to their charges.

It is sound strategy to come at relationships with the idea that we're not going to spend as much time confronting enemies as we are nurturing friends. It is foolish and futile to fret too much about detractors. Jesus had his; we'll probably have ours somewhere in our ministry. But confronting them, or even spending a lot of time with them, is not smart. We end up confronting enemies and mending fences when we should be loving friends and bolstering bridges.

When Jesus sent his first followers out on their mission of mercy, he told them to offer themselves to people with love and grace. But if their efforts were rejected, he told them to "shake the dust off their feet" and move on down the road. Somewhere down the road were people who would greet them with open arms and open hearts. In essence, he told those early followers to leave their detractors behind and go find friends.

• *Deal with the problem sooner rather than later.* We can save ourselves a ton of grief by dealing with problems early. It's a lot easier to deal with small problems early than it is to deal with big problems late. One reason we find ourselves in situations of conflict and confrontation is that we've allowed molehills to grow into mountains.

If only we had talked to the church secretary when we first sensed she was unhappy in her job, we might not be talking about her termination today. If only the church staff had gone out to eat together each week after our staff meeting, we might not be in such turmoil now. If only we had called our friend when we first sensed she was in trouble, we might not be so estranged today. If only . . . . If only . . . .

Hear Tom Peters once again: "Believe me on this: Most of the mistakes you will make in your career (and probably in your personal life) will come from having avoided that four-minute phone call that could have stopped the farmhand from letting out the cow that kicked over the lantern that started the fire that burned down the barn . . . ."[3]

Most of the mistakes we'll make in our church career are that way too. If we'll take care of the little problems early, we can avoid big problems later on. When it comes to conflict and confrontation, an ounce of prevention is worth at least a pound of cure.

• *Live above reproach.* We pastors can eliminate much conflict and confrontation simply by not giving people any ammunition for criticism. That is to say, we can eliminate *legitimate* criticism by being above reproach in our morals, commitment, and work ethic.

Sometimes we pastors need to be confronted. If we're cheating on our spouse, someone needs to call our hand and demand repentance. If we're "fudging" on our church expense account, the church treasurer needs to barge into our study and throw a tantrum. If we've grown lazy and undisciplined and spend more time on the golf course than in the study, it's legitimate for the personnel committee to complain. And if we've become "churchaholics" who judge our worth by how many hours we work and how many people show up for church on Sunday, our spouse has every right to tell us we've lost our way.

Sometimes confrontation is necessary, and sometimes we pastors need to be on the receiving end of it. But we can reduce criticism by actually practicing what we preach. We will *not* cheat on our spouse. We will *not* "fudge" on the expense account. We will *not* spend more time on the golf course than in the study. We will *not* become "churchaholics." We will *not* do anything, in fact, that will compromise our ministry or hurt our effectiveness for Christ.

That way, when people do come with a word of confrontation—our theology is misguided, our stance on some social issue is wrong, the music in the service was terrible, we didn't visit Aunt Bertha in the hospital, we're not friendly enough, and so on and so on—at least we'll know that when it comes to the pastoral issues that matter most, we're above reproach and not worthy of potshots.

Living above reproach won't eliminate "henpecking," but it will eliminate justified complaints.

The six things I've mentioned as part of my nonconfrontational leadership style are not revolutionary, but at least they're a starting place if you buy into the Confrontation Paradox. If you've discovered, like me, that confrontation is usually destructive and that it seldom confronts the problem, you will look for ways to be a good leader without doing much confrontation.

And when you do have to confront someone, you will do so with your eyes wide open, fully aware that confrontation often does more harm than good.

[1] Tom Peters, *The Pursuit of WOW!* (New York: Vintage Books, 1994), 51.

[2] Ibid., 51.

[3] Ibid., 52.

The Intimacy Paradox

Distance often helps people more than closeness.

Pastors are bridge-builders. You could make a strong case, I think, for the notion that building bridges is our first priority. We are called to build bridges between people and God. And we are called to build bridges between people and people.

That second part of our bridge-building function means we are constantly trying to create community among people. We endeavor to make our church "one in the Spirit, one in the Lord." We sing songs in our services about the church being "the family of God," and we repeatedly remind folks that we are "brothers and sisters in Christ." We also preach sermons about the "koinonia" that is supposed to exist among the people of God and how we Christians are supposed to love, encourage, forgive, and affirm one another.

This emphasis on Christians becoming "close" is, generally, a good and biblical one. No one wants to be in a church where people are estranged from one another and where there is no sense of community. We all want to be members of churches, and pastors of churches, where people love one another and are close to one another.

But our songs and sermons about community need to be tempered by the Intimacy Paradox: *Distance often helps people more than closeness.* Lest we start to deify closeness, we need to keep in mind that distance is not all bad. Distance gives people gifts that closeness can't. Too much closeness produces bad results in any group, including the church.

Let me count the ways:

• *Too much closeness scares some people away.* There is an undefined, unidentified subculture of people repelled by closeness. These people are loners . . . and proud of it! A writer named Anneli Rufus has written a book titled *Party of One (The Loners' Manifesto).* In it she tells us what it's like to be part of this subculture:

Loners are all types, subjective and objective thinkers, religious and atheist, soldiers and screenwriters and supermodels. We are the group that is never a group, that sneers at groups. In number theory, we might be described as "the set of units that are not associated with any other unit." We are the cofraternity whose members would rather chew Brillo pads than gather in some rathskeller to plan a strategy. We will never stage a protest march, a rally at which loners chorus, *Do not call us on the phone! Leave, leave us alone!* We cannot lend each other our support. It goes against our nature—in body, at least, if not in mind.[1]

The loner, she says, "swims alone through a sea of social types. Talkers. Lunchers. Touchers."

Now imagine such a person at church. This person is immediately descended upon by Christians determined to be friendly. Talkers. Lunchers. Touchers. Then this newcomer is invited to become a part of some group—a Sunday school class, the softball team, or the senior adult fellowship. If, by chance, this person should ever decide to join the church (which is unlikely), he or she has to walk an aisle, stand in front of the whole congregation, and then shake hands with dozens of friendly folks after the service.

Those of us on the giving end of the fellowship are just trying to be welcoming, to extend to this newcomer the offer of community. But we are assuming that everyone wants community, that closeness is appealing to all, when the truth is that some loner-types would prefer to be left alone.

These loners are not bad people. They're just "wired" a little differently than the majority of folks. And they deserve love, respect, and the good news of Jesus Christ.

One of the more intriguing, ignored issues facing the modern church is how to preach and teach the gospel to people who don't like to be in groups. Nearly everything we do in church assumes that closeness is next to godliness, so we have classes, groups, fellowships, teams, and corporate worship services. But the undefined, unidentified subculture of loners will not be attracted to these group activities, and they will secretly wonder if the church has anything at all to offer people like them. Talk of closeness will not attract them at all; it will scare them away.

• *Too much closeness stifles freedom.* My guess is the reason loners want to be left alone has something to do with freedom. They want to be free to think their own thoughts, free to spend their time they way they choose, free to live unencumbered by the demands and expectations of others. It is a healthy impulse, I think, and one most of us feel. That some people take the impulse to an extreme does-n't invalidate the impulse.

Too much closeness violates individuality. Too much togetherness makes people tired and saps their joy. That is why absence makes the heart grow fonder. When we have the privilege of experiencing the absence of someone, we can then better appreciate that person's presence. Distance often enhances relationships.

Occasionally, I start to feel overwhelmed by too many people, too many entries in the day planner, and too many thoughts in the brain. The closeness that comes from working with people, worshiping with people, ministering to people, and being available to people starts to wear me down. I start to feel bur-dened and un-free.

When that feeling of un-freedom starts to descend upon me, I know it is time to make a dash to Port Aransas, a sleepy little sea town just three hours down I-37. There Sherry and I are completely anonymous. No one knows or cares who we are. We put on old clothes, walk the beach in our shorts and flip-flops, eat at our favorite seafood place, sip coffee at a hole-in-the-wall pastry shop, read mystery novels, and watch the waves roll in. The anonymity and free-dom of Port Aransas recharges our batteries and makes us fit to come back to church life. From time to time, we have to get away from people, to abandon closeness for aloneness.

And we need to grant others in our church the same privilege. Too much closeness will produce a church of tired, un-free people.

• *Too much closeness inhibits vision.* Our church recently called a new staff member. I was eager for him to come on board because I wanted someone to look at our church through "new eyes." I wanted him to point out things the rest of us can no longer see.

Most of us no longer have "eyes to see" that the tile in the men's bathroom needs to be replaced ("Tile? We have tile in the men's bathroom?"), that our printed order of worship is confusing to visitors ("If it works for us, it ought to work for them too."), or that our nursery is not inviting to young families ("What's wrong with our nursery? We replaced the carpet in there just ten years ago!"). Our closeness to the institution and to one another inhibits our vision of how things really are.

The old joke that a camel is a horse designed by a committee has some truth to it. Committees and other groups typically lack the vision and imagination that only distance can bring. No wonder we keep producing camels around the church. We're all fused together in such a way that nobody can see clearly any-more. We're all nearly blind.

Maybe what we need to do is encourage some people in the church to distance themselves from us for a season. "Go out into the wilderness for a while," we could commission them, "and dream some dreams, see some visions. Then come back to us, energized and with new eyes, and tell us what you saw in the wilderness and what you see in our church. We're all stuck here in a sincere attempt to build community and foster closeness, and in the process we've lost our vision. Your assignment is to get above our stuckness and give us a fresh perspective on what you see God calling us to be and do."

That kind of vision doesn't usually come from the crowd. It comes from someone who has left the crowd to get an objective, imaginative perspective on things.

• *Too much closeness retards personal maturity.* A couple of chapters ahead, I write about the Self Paradox: *The best way to help others is to take care of yourself.* When we get to that paradox, I'm going to say that focusing on the group, or even focusing on another person, can do more harm than good to that group or individual. The best way for any of us to help others is to become people of substance and integrity ourselves, people in love with God and life. If we will get *our* act together, we just might have a shot at helping someone else. More on this paradox shortly.

But to become people in love with God and life who have a chance at helping others, we need to spend time alone. Yes, we need to be in community, too, so that we can learn how to love. But we also need time alone, time when we can decide who we are and how we're going to invest our lives. Too much closeness keeps us from coming face to face with ourselves and learning the hard truths that come only in private.

Have you ever noticed that the most pivotal moments in Jesus' life were those he spent alone? When he was tempted in the wilderness, he was alone. When he faced conflict and pressure in his ministry, he would go off by himself. When he faced his own death in the Garden of Gethsemane, he faced it alone. And when he hung on the cross, he did so alone, feeling forsaken by both God and people.

Why? Why would he journey through those difficult times by himself? I think it was because he *chose* to be alone. Deciding on his life's mission wasn't a committee affair. Being true to God in hard times wasn't something to be debated in the marketplace. Dying on a cross for the salvation of the world wasn't a topic he could put to vote among his friends. Those kinds of decisions demand solitude and the firm resolve that comes from spending time alone with God.

We too will have pivotal moments in our lives and ministries. At times, we'll feel like tossing in the towel and handing in our ordination papers. Or perhaps we'll pass through family or marital woes that make us miserable. Or maybe we'll have to deal with such agony in our family or church that we'll question both the goodness and providence of God.

When we arrive at those places, a good friend is fine to have, but, frankly, we'd better be prepared to be like Jesus and face our agony alone. Alone, we'll mature into the likeness of Christ. Alone, we'll get in touch with our deepest self. And alone we'll encounter a Presence who always comes to people one at a time.

What is true for us, of course, is true for everyone in our church, everyone in our sphere of influence. The people we love and to whom we minister need time alone. In our clamor for togetherness and closeness in church, let's not forget that there are some lessons in life and some experiences with God that come only when people get off by themselves, when they distance themselves from the herd.

You can probably guess from the four things I've just said about closeness that I'm not as quick to trumpet the necessity of intimacy at church as I used to be. We don't sing "The Family of God" as much as we once did. I sense that we church leaders often promise more than we can deliver. The truth is that, for most people, church won't be family; it will be church. They'll know some people at church, but not all. They'll like some people at church, but not all.

When we talk too much about everybody at church being close, we're almost guaranteeing that some people will become disillusioned: "The preacher keeps talking about this place being a family, but I haven't found a brother or sister yet. Maybe the church down the road can be my family." They didn't find it here, so they moved on.

In his book *Solitude,* Anthony Storr suggests that we put too much emphasis on "close relationships" in our culture: "The burden of value with which we are at present loading interpersonal relationships is too heavy for those fragile craft to carry. Our expectation that satisfying relationships should, ideally, provide happiness and that, if they do not, there must be something wrong with those relationships, seems to be exaggerated."[2]

If that expectation exists in the culture-at-large, it exists even more in the church. But if we're smart, we refuse to deify closeness. And we always keep in mind the gifts that distance bestows.

1 Anneli Rufus, *Party of One* (New York: Marlowe & Company, 2003), introduction, xxvii.

2 Anthony Storr, *Solitude* (New York: Free Press, 1988), introduction, xiii.

The Ministry Paradox

The more you try to help people,
the more helpless people become.

Susan used to call me at least once a week. Lately, she has stopped calling, and I can't say I'm sorry.

She would call to complain about the management at her apartment complex, criticize the government for not taking better care of people like her, tell me of her latest physical ailment, gripe about her abusive father, lambaste other churches for their insensitivity to her needs, and, primarily, ask for money from our church.

Susan has always had too much month left at the end of her disability check and constantly needs supplemental income. She's always dealing with a personal crisis: she can't pay her phone bill, the electric company is on the verge of turning off her power, or she doesn't have enough money to buy the expensive food she needs for her special diet.

So Susan calls me—or *did* call me—and our church has helped her on many occasions. Once, I even hand-delivered a check to her apartment complex because, after all, Susan is handicapped and can't drive. Other times, we've just put the check in the mail. I discovered in my conversations with Susan that ours is just one of many churches she calls for help. She is candid about her solicitation of churches.

What's a pastor to do about the Susans of the world? I'm convinced she is not a con artist. She really is handicapped. And she really does have more needs than she can take care of. But what I eventually realized over my months of conversing with Susan is that we weren't helping her. We were putting a band-aid on her problem, but we weren't really helping her.

In fact, we—no, let's get more honest and personal here—*I* was actually contributing to her helplessness. Dealing with Susan underscored again for me the truth of the Ministry Paradox: *The more you try to help people, the more helpless people become.*

Susan is the latest in a long line of helpless people I've tried to rescue. Before her there were Bobbie, Robert, Elizabeth, Sharon, Jim, Butch, Mary, and others I can't even remember. Looking back on it now, my ministry has been littered with stray puppies I've taken off the street and tried to help. So far, my batting average is only slightly better than zero.

In another book, written long before Susan and several others on my "stray puppy" list came along, I wrote:

> I have personally taken under wing several people whose lives obviously needed a major overhaul. I entered the reformation business with great confidence, certain that my shining example and profound words of counsel would work miracles. In my mind, I saw ugly caterpillars being transformed into glorious butterflies because of my influence.
>
> Alas, it was not to be. The caterpillars stayed caterpillars. My best efforts brought forth no butterflies. The reason for the failure, I see now, was that the transformation was *my* idea, *my* project. The caterpillars were quite content, thank you, with what they were. They had no desire to work, study, save money, seek forgiveness, or do any of the other difficult things that would make transformation possible. I have learned the hard way that personal change without personal motivation is impossible.[1]

The family systems people use two terms that are helpful when thinking about the Ministry Paradox: *underfunctioning* and *overfunctioning*. Understanding these terms can shed light on this paradox and also keep us from inadvertently enabling helpless people to become even more helpless.

The people on my list of stray puppies have one thing in common: they are all *underfunctioners*. They live beneath their potential and assume too little responsibility for their lives. They exemplify the classic symptoms of people who underfunction:

- *Lack of organization.* Their organizational skills are minimal and maybe nonexistent. Their lives are in shambles, as are their cars and places of residence. They just can't "get their act together" and feel constantly confused and out of control.
- *Money problems.* Perhaps because they are so disorganized, underfunctioners have a lot of money woes. And when they do get money, they often "blow it" on unnecessary purchases.
- *Panic under stress.* Stressful situations send underfunctioners into panic, and they tend to cycle downward when pressure comes into their lives. When they come or call looking for help, there is a frantic urgency to their requests.

- *Chronic irresponsibility.* Their underfunctioning has become a way of life. They are known to their families and friends as "the problem," "the irresponsible one," "the sick one," "the fragile one," or a similar designation. In essence, underfunctioners have a life script that tells them to live beneath their potential.
- *Frequent physical or mental illness.* These people tend to develop physical or mental symptoms that are genuine and ongoing. Their underfunctioning sets in motion a chain of events that leads them away from wholeness and health.
- *Asking for advice or rescue.* When independent thought or action is required, underfunctioners turn instead to others for help. They lack the confidence or the skills to handle situations, so they consistently run to others to be rescued.

Susan has all of those characteristics. So do most of the others I've tried to help through the years. And, as I said, I have had the feeling that my attempts to help have served only to cement these people in their underfunctioning. I have dutifully played my role in their sad life script.

So I (and most pastors, I would guess) have been known to overfunction. At least at certain times with certain people, I've displayed the classic symptoms of the overfunctioner:

- *Knowing what's best for others.* Overfunctioners have a clear picture of what's best not only for themselves but also for other people. Overfunctioners have the motivation to change themselves and to effect change in those around them. If only the people around them had as much motivation as they do . . . .
- *Moving in quickly to advise, rescue, and take over when stress hits.* Overfunctioners are quick to step in when trouble comes. They plan, organize, and act. They've even been known to do for others what others should be doing for themselves. That's why they're called *over*functioners.
- *Feeling responsible for others.* Overfunctioners are usually caring people. The reason they think they know what's best for others and the reason they are quick to the rescue is that they genuinely care. They are other-centered to an extreme and feel responsible for the welfare of others. They feel so responsible, though, that they venture where they shouldn't go.
- *Worrying more than necessary.* It's a heavy load overfunctioners feel called to bear: not only are they responsible for their own welfare, they're also responsible for the welfare of their spouse, children, coworkers, neighbors, and parishioners. That's quite a load to carry, and that heavy load translates into a lot of worry. Overfunctioners worry more than they should.

- *Experiencing periodic burnout or depression.* There are two reasons overfunctioners burn out or get depressed. First, they've accumulated a high level of anxiety through the years. It's not easy taking care of everybody else's business. Second, they don't take adequate care of themselves. They are so busy putting out fires in other people's lives that they don't tend to their own.
- *Invulnerability.* Overfunctioners often have a hard time sharing their own vulnerable, underfunctioning side. They are looked upon as people who are "strong," who "have it all together." They are reluctant to display even the slightest chink in their armor of strength.

I think most pastors are overfunctioners. We were attracted to the ministry precisely because we have it in us to help others. But in a sincere desire to help others, we sometimes accidentally cross into overfunctioning. When we cross that line, we fall headlong into the dastardly Ministry Paradox: *The more you try to help people, the more helpless they become.* Our ministry unintentionally starts to feed sickness.

In light of the Ministry Paradox, then, here are a few thoughts to consider:

- *First, underfunctioners will always seek out overfunctioners.* Susan and I belong together: she's the classic underfunctioner; I'm the classic overfunctioner. In ministry, as in love, opposites attract.

Right now, Susan is no longer calling. But looking back on my track record, I'm going to guess that even if she never calls again, another Susan will come along to take her place. I attract Susans like my garage attracts clutter.

It works out well for both parties. The Susans need me so they can remain stuck in their underfunctioning. Sadly, I need them so I can remain stuck in my overfunctioning. We all feel more comfortable when we're living out our life script.

- *Second, when it comes to helping others, grow accustomed to the gray.* By that I mean there is no easy answer to this underfunctioning/overfunctioning dilemma, and there is a lot of gray in ministering to others. Helping people is not a black and white proposition.

On one hand, I can't refuse to help people just because I might overfunction. Some people really need help. Some people have legitimate needs. To turn a deaf ear to all requests for aid, or to declare everyone who calls wanting help an underfunctioner, is a cop-out and a betrayal of ministry. On the other hand, I do need to know about the Ministry Paradox. I do need to know that I can unintentionally do more harm than good when I don my cape and run to the rescue of people in trouble. Some help is nothing more than me feeding someone else's dysfunction while inflating my own ego.

So we grow accustomed to the gray of the ministerial life. We know that we have to take risks to help people. But we also know that helping people who refuse to help themselves is really no help at all. We live with the tension of ministry: we help, but we don't help too much.

Blessed and rare is the minister who can walk that precarious tightrope.

• *Third, remember the ultimate goal of ministry.* My ultimate goal for Susan is not to pay her light bill every month. That might be a noble short-term goal, but it isn't the final answer for her. The ultimate goal is to enable her to become mature—mature in her relationship with God and people and mature in terms of her own functioning.

If my help to any person doesn't contribute to that person's maturity, it isn't really help. If my help is contributing to a person's immaturity, I need to quit helping that person. Promoting underfunctioning is not exactly wise ministry.

That's why the Ministry Paradox is important to know. It reminds us that there is *real* help that actually helps and *pseudo*-help that actually hurts.

• *Fourth, when it comes to real ministry, less is better.* The Ministry Paradox is a caution light that invites us to slow down and notice which people we're actually helping. It beckons us to consider carefully the help we're giving people so we can use our time and talents most productively.

If we determine that some of our help is perpetuating a lifestyle of helplessness in those people, we quit. If, on the other hand, we determine that our help is producing maturity in people, we renew our zeal and double our efforts. But it calls for discernment to see where maturity is happening and where it isn't.

We can't help everyone. As much as we overfunctioners would like to, we simply can't help all people with all their problems. So we learn to be selective. And we learn that when it comes to effective ministry, less is better. Better to pour our efforts into a few lives moving toward maturity than to scatter shoot at dozens of people who will stay stuck in underfunctioning.

Jesus gave himself primarily to twelve people. He knew that saving the whole world depended on his focused love for twelve men. That is not a bad strategy for modern pastors to emulate.

---

[1] Judson Edwards, *Regaining Control of Your Life* (Minneapolis: Bethany House, 1989), 109.

The Helper's Paradox

*The best way to take care of others
is to take care of yourself.*

There is an old joke about two men who sat together on an airplane.

"Are you a minister?" one asked the other.

"No," the other replied. "I've just had the flu for a couple of weeks."

It's a common notion, really—ministers are frail, pale, and wimpy. Worn out from service to God and others. Weak and weary from a life of sacrifice. Poor, pitiful pastors depriving themselves for a higher calling and looking like sickly flu victims in the process.

It is also a *false* notion, or should be, because ministering from a stance of personal deprivation is both foolish and ineffective. That is why the Helper's Paradox is important to remember: *The best way to take care of others is to take care of yourself.*

At first blush, the Helper's Paradox sounds like narcissism: pastors, like the rest of society, deciding to look out for number one. Pastors opting out of other-centeredness to focus on self-centeredness.

But that's not what the Helper's Paradox is about at all. This paradox recognizes that we can't give to others something we don't have ourselves. It reminds us that all of those wonderful fruits of the spirit—love, joy, peace, patience, and so on—are not so much *taught* as *caught*. In other words, the Helper's Paradox is a stark reminder that ministry has more to do with who we are than what we say or do.

We can work sixty hours a week, visit the sick religiously, burn midnight oil preparing homiletical masterpieces, and meet with committees until our tongues hang out, but if we're tired, depleted, discouraged, and "flu-like," it profiteth us nothing. People will be more influenced by our spirit—the life and energy in us—than by our deeds.

That is why it is imperative that we take care of ourselves, keep our inner batteries charged, and find ways to stay physically, emotionally, and spiritually energized. If we really believe that Jesus came to give people abundant life and if we preach that to the people in the pews on Sunday morning, it behooves us to believe that Jesus came to give *us* abundant life too. We really can't expect others to be any more relaxed, fun-loving, or alive than we are.

With that truth in mind, let me tell you more about my Thursdays.

As I mentioned earlier, I take every Thursday off and spend it doing relaxing, fun-loving, coming-alive kinds of activities. It is not stretching the truth to say that Thursdays have probably saved my ministry. Without that day away from church and ministerial duties, I might be selling insurance or driving a taxicab by now.

Here is a typical Thursday:

I wake up between 5:30 and 6:00, as is my daily custom, to drink coffee and read the paper. Even on my day off, I can't "sleep in," so I enjoy an hour of solitude just sipping coffee and perusing the sports page.

At 7:30, I head toward the tennis courts. Every Thursday, I play doubles with my "old guys," three retired men who play tennis several times a week. We always have spirited play and lots of fun and laughter. After tennis, we go to a local bagels place for a cup of coffee.

Then I go home and work in the yard a while. In Texas, we have to do yard work seven months a year, so most Thursdays I need to mow, edge, sweep, or putter in the flower beds.

After yard work, I shower and put on some old, comfortable clothes. Then Sherry and I go out to eat—maybe to Sarita's if we're hungry for Mexican food, or Taipei if Chinese strikes our fancy, or The Brown Bag if we want a sandwich. We eat out just about every Thursday lunch and have been known to drive across San Antonio to try a new spot.

Then, it's on to HEB, our local grocery store, where we do our weekly shopping. Sherry always plans a week's worth of meals—from Thursday to Thursday—and has a list of groceries needed to make those meals happen. We obsessively follow our list, checking off items as we toss them into our grocery cart. Then we grimace as we come to the checkout, knowing we have to pay for all the stuff we've accumulated.

After our grocery expedition, we go home, put the groceries away, and launch into making our soup of the week. We try a different soup each week and usually cook the soup together. I chop, Sherry mixes. Or I mix, she chops. However we do it, when we get through we have a pot of delicious soup we can eat on all week.

Then it's naptime, or reading time, or run-down-to-the-hardware-store time before we cook dinner and settle in for the evening. The evening might be watching the Spurs on television, making a jaunt to Borders for book-browsing and coffee, or just hanging around the house.

By bedtime, we're deliciously relaxed and tired from a day of fun activities. We might read before we drift off to sleep, sorry that Thursday is gone, but better prepared to face whatever Friday might bring.

That's the way it goes most Thursdays. No church. Nothing religious at all. Just life in all of its simple glory. Coffee and the paper. Tennis. The old guys. Lunch on the town. Grocery shopping. Making soup. Browsing the bookstore. Falling asleep. Nothing spectacular. But nothing to be taken for granted either.

Without Thursday, I wouldn't be much of a pastor.

Those unspectacular Thursdays keep me alive. Without them, I would be too religious, too institutional, and too uptight. I need one day to be human, one day to push a grocery cart and walk the world in Bermuda shorts and flip-flops. And the better I feel and the happier I am, the better pastor I am.

I know the Helper's Paradox is true because I've tried it both ways. I've tried being religious, uptight, and worn out. And I've tried being human, relaxed, and refreshed. Human, relaxed, and refreshed is better. I can take better care of people, be a better pastor to people, when I take care of myself.

Every day I do battle with my day planner. The temptation is always to become over-committed, over-involved, and over-stressed, to buy into the idea that I must be all things to all people and solve the problems of the whole world. The temptation is to take care of everything *out there* and nothing *in here*.

But being faithful means we find what we're here on earth to take care of and then focus on those things. If I'm going to win that daily war with the day planner and take care of myself, I need to remember exactly what I'm here to take care of.

Years ago, I wrote down what I felt God was calling me to do, five priorities that would define me and dictate what I wrote in that day planner. These five priorities have never changed, and remembering them still enables me to be faithful and to take care of myself:

(1) *Family.* When I first listed "family" as one of my priorities, my children, Stacy and Randel, were small. I knew, though, that I didn't want to sacrifice them on the altar of ministerial success. So I went to all of their sports activities and even coached some of their teams. Sherry and I were active booster club members and worked our turns in the concession stand. I put "family stuff" over "church stuff" and have never regretted it.

Now that Stacy and Randel are grown and gone from home, they are still objects of our concentrated attention. They both live in Austin, just two hours from us, and we get to visit often. We also talk on the phone and e-mail each other frequently.

And now that our children are out on their own, Sherry and I have a lot of time together. One reason Thursday is such a delightful day is that we get to spend nearly the whole day together doing things we both enjoy. It's a day of focused attention on one another.

(2) *Being a pastor.* I have been a pastor for thirty years now. For twenty-seven of those years, I have served two churches. Frankly, I've had moments when other pursuits looked awfully inviting. I thought once of opening a bookstore and another time probed the possibility of running a bed-and-breakfast. But those were momentary fantasies fueled by unpleasant situations. I've never *seriously* considered being anything but a pastor.

Since being a pastor is part of who I am and who I am called to be, the church stakes a large claim on my time. That means a sizeable chunk of my life is given to studying, preaching, counseling, visiting people in the hospital, attending committee meetings, planning worship services, writing articles, meeting with our church staff, and other less glamorous duties too numerous to mention.

(3) *Writing.* I can't be "me" without trying to express my "insides" on paper. E. B. White once described writing as an affliction, "something that rises up on you, as a welt."[1] For better or worse, I have the affliction and spend a good bit of time writing, editing, sending out query packages, and trying to bandage my ego when publishers reject my stuff. I also lead a couple of writers' conferences each year.

I'm not a particularly disciplined writer. I don't write every day, for example, or set goals for how many pages I'll write each week. But seldom does a week go by that I haven't hurled words at paper to see if any of them make sense. For me, writing is an affliction that isn't going away any time soon.

(4) *Reading.* I am a self-confessed "bookaholic." Books give me hours of enjoyment. They feed my spirit. They give me ideas for preaching. For me, the only thing better than wandering through a bookstore for hours is actually finding a book there that will transport me to another world.

Because books are so important to my personal growth, I am reading something all the time. The lamp stand by my bed has four books on it right now: a murder mystery, a baseball book, a book about a guy who rebuilt an old truck, and a book on why Americans are experiencing more and more success but enjoying it less and less. I don't think I can stretch my mind or have much to say if I don't read.

(5) *Exercise.* For fifteen years, I ran three miles almost every day. I was an avid runner and even completed a marathon. Now my knees are shot, and I've moved on to other less punishing forms of exercise. As I mentioned, I play tennis every week, and I also work out at a fitness center three times a week. Sherry and I walk a lot, too, so just about every day I'm getting some kind of exercise.

I realized early on that if my ministry was going to have any vitality at all, my body would have to have vitality. I knew I needed to exercise, eat right, get plenty of sleep, and generally behave as if my body is the temple of God. That was true when I decided on these five priorities years ago, and it is still true today.

When I look at the five priorities I pinpointed early in my ministry, I'm struck by two thoughts: First, I realize how unspectacular they are. If they in any way are a plan for changing the world, they are a modest plan. No, let me rephrase that: a *very* modest plan. There's nothing earthshaking about focusing on family, being a pastor, writing, reading, and exercising. But the second thing I realize is how true they still are for me. Over the years, these five priorities have remained constant. I've set my sail by them and planned my days around them. As unspectacular as they are, they're still my guiding lights. If I can take care of these things, give my best time and effort to these five priorities, I will call myself faithful. And I will be taking care of myself, so I can then take care of others.

What is important about my list is that, in addition to giving me a strategy for doing battle with my day planner, it reminds me that "being a pastor" is only one of my five priorities. "Being a pastor" is an important part of my identity, but it isn't the totality of who I am. I have a life, an identity, apart from the church.

If for some reason I'm taken out of my role as pastor of a Baptist church, I won't collapse in despair. I'm more than a pastor. I'm also a husband and father, a writer, a reader, and someone intent on staying in good physical shape. Take away my pulpit, and I'll still be calling my kids on the phone and taking Sherry out for Thursday lunch, I'll still be flailing away at my computer writing books and articles, I'll still be reading voraciously and prowling bookstores, and I'll still be playing tennis with my "old guys" and getting up early to lift weights at the fitness center. Take away one part of my identity, and I'll still have four other parts.

As a pastor, I must make sure I have a "self." I must work to be an authentic human being who loves God, people, and life. I must never mistake my role as a pastor as my sole identity. Being a pastor is a high calling and a precious privilege, but it isn't "me." My "me" is bigger than that.

The more I can take care of that real "me" and remain faithful to my priorities, the better I'll do as a pastor.

I guess these are the ultimate paradoxes for pastors: The less we're consumed by being a pastor, the better pastor we will be. And we can't be a true pastor to others until we first learn to be a pastor to ourselves.

[1] E. B. White, *One Man's Meat* (New York: Harper & Row, 1938), 254.

The Organization Paradox

*The more organized the church
becomes, the less it accomplishes.*

Those of us who are pastors work in what the world calls "organized religion." We are commonly viewed as corporate executives of an organized religious enterprise. But on our more honest (cynical?) days, we would rise up against both of those terms and adamantly declare that our enterprise is neither organized nor religious.

We would declare first that we don't peddle "religion." If anything, we preach the *end* of religion. Listen to Robert Capon in his book *The Mystery of Christ*:

> Christianity is the proclamation of the end of religion, not of a new religion, or even of the best of all religions. And therefore if the cross is the sign of anything, it's the sign that God has gone out of the religion business and solved all the world's problems without requiring a single human being to do a single religious thing. What the cross is actually a sign of is the fact that religion can't do a thing about the world's problems—that it never did work and it never will . . . .[1]

Since God opted out of the religion business, so do we.

We would also declare that we're not too keen on being "organized." And we would make that declaration because of the next paradox I want you to ponder: *The more organized the church becomes, the less it accomplishes.*

It takes only a cursory glance at church organizational structure to notice we have borrowed that structure not from a *biblical* model, but from a *business* model. The biblical model provides almost no organizational structure at all. The early church wasn't a business—no buildings, no paid employees, no hierarchical management pyramids, no advertising, no formal organization of any kind. The early church was all about people. It was *personal,* not *institutional.*

But the modern church has taken its cue from the corporate world. Like big business, we have buildings, budgets, bylaws, bank accounts, and bureaucracy. The church has organized itself by the business model, which means the pastor has been designated as the resident CEO. For some of us, it's a designation we neither desire nor enjoy.

Of course, the church needs *some* degree of organization. Paul's letters to the Corinthian church remind us what happens when there is no organization in the church and people try to exist together with no structure. The result is chaos and ineffectiveness.

But my guess is that, in our day, for every church that is ineffective because of *too little* organization, twenty others are ineffective because of *too much* organization. In a legitimate desire to be organized and efficient, we've gone too far and over-organized ourselves into a policy-ridden bureaucracy.

Three bad things happen when a church gets afflicted with too much organization:

First, the church becomes mesmerized by maintenance. In *Orbiting the Giant Hairball,* Gordon McKenzie tells a story about an experience his father had when he was ten years old. His father was visiting a cousin who lived in the country, and, to impress his visitor from the city, the cousin offered to show him a neat trick.

"Do you know how to mesmerize a chicken?" he asked.

"Mesmerize? Uh-uh. What's that?"

"Follow me."

The cousin led the way to a ramshackle chicken coop out behind the farmhouse. He selected a fine, white hen, put it under his arm, and marched to the front of the house. Then he took a piece of chalk and drew a line on the porch. He stood the hen over the chalk line and held her beak to it. After a little while, the boy slowly removed his hands, but the hen remained motionless, hypnotized by the chalk line. Cousin had mesmerized a chicken.

"Let's do another one. Let's do another one," McKenzie's father pleaded.

And so they did. They mesmerized one chicken after another, until the chicken coop was empty and the front porch was filled with motionless chickens with their beaks on the chalk line.

After telling that story, McKenzie draws this conclusion:

The same thing that happened to those chickens can happen to you. When you join an organization, you are, without fail, taken by the back of the neck and pushed down and down until your beak is on a line—not a chalk line, but a company line. And the company line says things like: *"This is our history. This is our philosophy. These are our policies. These are our procedures. These are our politics. This is simply the way we are."* If you are not careful, you will be hypnotized by this line. And what a pity if that happens.[2]

I would like to believe that our churches are not that "mesmerizing." I don't really believe we grab people by the neck and force them to do things our way. But I also fear that we do sometimes say to people, perhaps unintentionally: *This is our church history. This is our church philosophy. Here is a copy of our church policies. These are the procedures we follow around here. And you'll quickly discover our church politics. This is simply the way we are. Welcome to our church!*

We can become so "organized" that we fixate on philosophies, policies, procedures, and politics and lose sight of people. Tragically, we create this ecclesiastical "hairball" and then have to spend most of our time taking care of it. Meetings. Policies. Bylaws. Amending the bylaws. Staff performance reviews. Expense account forms. Business meetings. And so on, ad nauseum. It all seems so necessary and important, but it's all about *maintenance,* not *ministry.*

That's the problem with organization. The more organized our churches become, the more time and effort we have to spend maintaining that organization. Every new layer on the "hairball" requires a committee or staff person to oversee it. We get trapped in a *maintenance* mode when we're called to be in a *ministry* mode.

Second, too much organization stems from, and leads to, lack of trust. In *Management of the Absurd,* Richard Farson told about a management consultant who led a group of managers in an exercise to design a low-trust organization. He wanted them to list all the things they would do and procedures they would institute to destroy trust and sabotage morale in an organization.

The managers had no trouble in generating a number of ideas:

Make sure that everything is locked up. Install time clocks. Introduce voluminous manuals of operating procedures. Develop rules and regulations on everything. Fire people without warning. Keep thick personnel folders on people to which they have no access. Hold private meetings to which most people are not admitted. And so on. One by one, the managers in the audience flushed with embarrassment and amusement as they recognized that they were describing aspects of their own organizations.[3]

Though we're hesitant to admit it, we often create exactly that kind of atmosphere in the church. Under the guise of "getting organized," "being responsible stewards," or "becoming more efficient," we do things that show we simply don't trust each other. We create "low trust" organizations in which no one feels the freedom to freelance or be creative. We have a policy or procedure for everything, and woe to the people who raise their heads from the chalk line.

One can only imagine what an over-organized, low-trust early church might have been like:

- Peter couldn't have preached at Pentecost until he was approved and accredited by the Personnel Committee.
- The disciples couldn't have healed anyone until given sanction and approval by the Health and Safety Committee.
- No one could have given money to help a hurting friend unless the expenditure was approved by the Finance Committee.
- No "signs and wonders" would have been allowed unless first approved by the church council.

Nobody could have done much of anything because "the organization" would have gummed up the works and made spontaneous action impossible. Over-organization would have robbed the early Christians of their vitality by creating an atmosphere of distrust and supervision. One line in the *Tao Te Ching* says, "The more prohibitions you have, the less virtuous people will be."[4] Ironically, the more we distrust each other, the more distrustful we all become.

Too much organization can set in motion a cycle of distrust that makes everyone in the church feel restricted and fearful. Unlike our early church ancestors, we're afraid to do anything spontaneous or creative. We keep our heads glued to the chalk line.

Third, too much organization saps the spirit of church leaders. Is there anything more discouraging and draining that managing a "hairball"? Can you think of a worse way to spend your time than enforcing policies, writing procedures, or keeping tabs on someone else's vacation time? Is there anything more fruitless that attending a bunch of committee meetings that are all about the "hairball"?

It sounds like the job from hell, but it is the very job many pastors find themselves doing. We thought we signed on to preach, pray, and pastor, only to discover that we're actually managers of an ecclesiastical business endeavor. Like the enterprise we lead, we pastors get stuck in maintenance duties when we're called to do ministry duties.

When I was a seminary student, a pastor told me I could succeed in the ministry if I could say "yes" to the following two questions: "Can you preach? And do you love people?" Since I thought I could become at least an adequate preacher and since I did love people, I felt buoyed by his words. I was on the right track.

But that pastor's counsel seems somehow dated and irrelevant in today's world. Pastor search committees are thrilled if a candidate can preach and if that candidate loves people, but there are other, more pressing questions that need to be asked today: "Are you a good leader? Can you run an organization? Can you make a church grow? Do you have organizational skills? Do you have a forceful personality? Can you manage people?"

Those are reasonable questions to ask a prospective pastor, I suppose, but they show the shift that has taken place in recent years. In our thinking about pastors, we've moved from a spiritual model (preaching well and loving people) to a managerial model (running a successful religious enterprise).

That shift saps the vitality of all pastors who are not managerial types. We find ourselves doing things we're not good at, and we find church members expecting us to do things that have nothing to do with what we think is legitimate ministry. We're expected to be managers, promoters, salespeople, and psychologists, but we keep hanging on to the antiquated notion of wanting to be a *pastor*, for God's sake (and for our own sanity's sake!).

When reflective people who feel called of God to be pastors wind up managing a "hairball," they are destined for major frustration. They will come home from church some Sundays wondering why in the world they opted to be a pastor when they could have been something like a forest ranger. In fact, after a long committee meeting or particularly rancorous session of the church council, they might even call around to see if there might be a forest ranger's job available somewhere. Anything would have to be more fun and fulfilling than managing that ecclesiastical "hairball."

So the question can appropriately be posed, how do you know if your church has too much organization? If too much organization is a bad thing, how do you know when your church has crossed the line and become over-organized? I would say to check the three effects I've mentioned in this chapter.

If your church has adopted a maintenance mentality, if you spend most of your time and effort on maintenance instead of ministry, you've crossed the line.

If there is a lack of spontaneity and trust in the church, if people don't feel free to try news things for fear of being "out of regulation," you've crossed the line.

And if the church staff and key lay leaders are drained and discouraged from running on the maintenance treadmill, you've crossed the line.

If your church has those three characteristics, you've organized yourselves into ineffectiveness. You've become "mesmerized" by organization, and somebody needs to shake you and wake you up.

[1] Robert Capon, *The Mystery of Christ* (Grand Rapids: Eerdmans, 1993), 62.

[2] Gordon McKenzie, *Orbiting the Giant Hairball* (New York: Viking, 1996), 51-53.

[3] Richard Farson, *Management of the Absurd* (New York: Simon & Schuster, 1996), 131.

[4] Stephen Mitchell, translator, *Tao Te Ching* (New York: Harper & Row, 1988), 57.

The Problems Paradox

Problems are not really problems at all.

I've often thought that when I retire from a life of being a pastor, I'm going to open a radio repair shop. In my "next life," I'd like to do something that allows me to see the results of my labor. At the end of the day, I want to be able to point to a couple of radios and say, "Those weren't working this morning, but now, because I put my hand and expertise to them, they work like new." Maybe that's why I take such crazy delight in mowing grass. When I get through, I can see the difference I've made.

Certainly, ministry is not like that. Most days, I go home not certain I've "fixed" anything or made much of a difference anywhere. Oh, I might have attended a few meetings, made a couple of hospital visits, tried to do a little sermon preparation, and talked to people on the phone. But there's nothing I can point to and say, "I fixed those today."

The reason for that, I've decided, is that we pastors don't actually deal with fixable problems. Richard Farson made a distinction that accurately describes pastoral work:

> One of the most valuable lessons, among many valuable lessons, I learned from philosopher Abraham Kaplan is to distinguish between a problem and a predicament. Problems can be solved; predicaments can only be coped with. Most of the affairs of life, particularly the most intimate and important ones, such as marriage and child rearing, are complicated, inescapable dilemmas— predicaments where no options look very good or better than any other. I believe that is true of management as well.[1]

I believe it's true of being a pastor, for sure. So let's add to our arsenal of paradoxes the Problems Paradox: *Problems are not really problems at all.* Knowing about this paradox can keep us from losing our sanity. It can also make us feel better as we drive home from a day at the church feeling we haven't accomplished a thing.

The truth is, we're not dealing with problems at all; we're dealing with predicaments. And those predicaments are "complicated, inescapable dilemmas where no options look very good or better than any other."

Let me tell you what's "on my plate" today, not because it's so impressive or unusual, but because it's so ordinary and usual. And probably because it's so typical of what you find on your pastoral "plate" many days.

- I'm preparing a funeral message for a good friend who died of cancer two days ago in Houston. I've talked to his wife on the phone and will help with the memorial service in a couple of days.
- I'm dealing with a couple in our church who are in their nineties and trying to cope with a host of "issues." She recently had a stroke and is under hospice care. He's at her side daily, watching and waiting.
- I just got off the phone with a woman in our church waiting for hip replacement surgery. She's in pain and frustrated that her doctors are so insensitive to her needs. Meanwhile, she waits in her assisted living facility hoping for something good to happen.
- I visited today with a woman undergoing chemotherapy and having a terrible time with nausea. She's been in the hospital for two weeks just trying to survive her treatments. She's not sure which is worse—the cancer or the chemotherapy.
- I talked yesterday with a family whose beloved wife and mother is going to have to go to an Alzheimer's facility near our church. She's been deteriorating rapidly, and her family can no longer take care of her.

As pastor to these people, I'm trying to support and love them in their stressful situations. But when I look at these five crises, I realize the one common thread that runs through them all is their "unfixability." These people don't have problems; they have predicaments. There's nothing I can do to fix these situations or make things a whole lot better. My friend has died. The old couple must wait for the inevitable at the hospice. The woman must endure her pain while hoping for a new hip. The woman undergoing chemotherapy will continue to suffer while she battles her cancer. The family enduring the agony of checking a loved one into the Alzheimer's place can't avoid the pain.

Welcome to the real world. And welcome to the world of the pastor, who deals with predicaments that can't be solved, only endured. But, with the strength and grace God gives, perhaps they can be endured with something less than despair.

Farson went on to say, "Predicaments require interpretive thinking. Dealing with a predicament demands the ability to put a larger frame around a situation, to understand it in its many contexts, to appreciate the deeper and often paradoxical causes and consequences. Alas, predicaments cannot be handled smoothly."[2]

I want you to notice the second sentence in that paragraph because I think it puts pastoral work in its proper perspective: *Dealing with a predicament demands the ability to put a larger frame around a situation, to understand it in its many contexts, to appreciate its deeper and often paradoxical causes and consequences.*

Pastors are called to use "interpretive thinking" to help people in three ways:

First, pastors help people put a larger frame around a situation. That, it could be argued, is the goal of all good pastoral care: to enable people to see a larger frame, to remind people of the transcendent in the midst of their predicament, to whisper the good news of a resurrection beyond every cross. We pastors don't have the power to remove crosses, but we do have the power to offer hope of resurrections.

When I go to Houston to lead the memorial service, that's what I'll try to do. I'll speak a biblical word that I hope will put a "larger frame" around my friend's life and death.

When I visit the old couple at the hospice, I'll try to remind them that she has lived a long and good life, that God has blessed them richly, and that they have every reason to believe that God's blessings will not cease at her death.

When I talk with the wonderful woman waiting for the hip replacement, I'll offer her hope that better days are coming, but I'll also assure her that God and God's people won't desert her even if she can't get her new hip. I'll try to lift her eyes beyond her pain to see the Help she has.

When I talk to the woman struggling through chemotherapy, I'll offer her my help and presence whenever she needs it. And I'll remind her that, even if she doesn't survive this struggle with cancer, she's in the hands of One who loves her.

When I deal with that family having to put their wife and mother in the Alzheimer's facility, I'll promise to visit her regularly and to make sure our church doesn't forget her in her new home. I'll also try to remind them that she is still the Beloved of God and that removing her from their home doesn't remove her from God's care.

In every one of those predicaments, I'll try to lift people's eyes to the hills, to remind them that ultimately their help comes from God, the maker of heaven and earth. I'll try to put a "larger frame" around their experience.

Second, pastors help people understand life in its many contexts. Pastors aren't answer-people, tossing proof texts at confused and predicament-riddled searchers. We're honest people who know that life is tough, God mysterious, and answers hard to come by, but that the spiritual dimension of human life must not be forgotten or ignored. We try to get people to put their experiences in the context of God's providence and love.

When I think of those pastoral care situations I'm dealing with right now, I realize all of the different contexts in which those people must try to interpret their predicaments.

They have to process their experience *physically.* They're grieving. They're hurting. They're losing weight. Or their bodies are changing in some significant, probably negative way.

They have to process their experience *emotionally.* They'll cry, feel numb, lash out in anger, or withdraw into a personal tomb of their own making.

They have to process their experience *relationally.* They have spouses, children, grandchildren, friends, and other loved ones who are being affected by their predicament. They have to figure out ways to love these people, even help these people through their grief, because they understand they don't suffer alone.

They have to process their experience *financially.* Hospital or hospice bills must be paid. Funerals must be arranged and paid for. New living quarters have to be found. Predicaments have a way of becoming expensive.

Finally, they have to process their experience *spiritually.* Predicaments also have a way of forcing people to ponder God and their relationship to God. My friend who just died called two weeks ago to say good-bye and to affirm his faith in the goodness of God and life. His crisis enabled him to lift his eyes to the hills. As pastors, we help people remember this spiritual context in the midst of their predicament.

Pastors know that predicaments force people to look at all of these factors and to see the many different contexts in which they live. And if pastors have a particularly close relationship with these people, they can walk with them as they traverse the contexts of their lives.

Third, pastors help people appreciate that life is full of paradoxical causes and consequences. This book is a testimony to the idea that a life of ministry is a life of paradox. But, in reality, life itself is full of paradoxes, and when people have to deal with frustrating predicaments, those paradoxes become evident. Some of the paradoxes discovered in the midst of predicaments are horrible and heartbreaking:

- The people you can least bear to lose are the ones who die first.
- The most religious people you know turn out to be the ones who help you least.
- The money you saved for the vacation has to go toward the funeral.
- In your suffering, your cherished theology profits you little.
- When you were having fun, time flew. Now, in your misery, time crawls.

The list of horrible, heartbreaking paradoxes is endless, and you can no doubt provide more examples from your own ministry.

But some of the paradoxes discovered in the midst of predicaments are gratifying and even life-changing:

- God seems clearer in the dark of suffering than in the light of happiness.
- Hope comes from the smallest of experiences and observations.
- Help comes from the strangest, most unlikely people.
- Most of what you thought was essential to your joy is not essential at all.
- Answers from God are overrated. What you need is the presence of God.
- The most significant moments in your life are insignificant moments.

Pastors know these things and can affirm them to people discovering them in their predicaments.

Those three facets of pastoral work arise out of the Problems Paradox. Once we know that *problems are not really problems at all,* that people are trapped in predicaments, we can go about the true business of pastoral care: (1) helping them put their situations into a larger frame, (2) encouraging them to sort through the various contexts of their predicament, and (3) inviting them to embrace the paradoxes they'll discover.

I do want you to pay special attention to one sentence in Farson's quote. He said, "Alas, predicaments cannot be handled smoothly."[3] The bad news is that we pastors aren't destined for smooth sailing. Helping people deal with predicaments isn't easy work. But the good news is that we don't have to feel particularly guilty when we go home feeling unfulfilled and ineffective.

We're dealing with people, not radios, and people are too complicated to be fixed.

[1] Richard Farson, *Management of the Absurd* (New York: Simon & Schuster, 1996), 42.

[2] Ibid., 43.

[3] Ibid., 43.

The Time Paradox

The less important the issue, the more time you will spend on it.

I still remember with horror a church business meeting I moderated years ago. Our church needed to buy folding chairs for the fellowship hall, and one of our committees brought a recommendation that we buy 100 chairs. It seemed like an innocuous, "slam-dunk" kind of recommendation.

But someone in the meeting brought a counter-proposal: Our church is going to grow, he asserted, and 100 chairs won't be enough. He moved that we buy 120 chairs. The maker of the original motion defended his number of 100. The counter-proposer defended his idea of 120. And, perhaps because of my brilliant moderating skills, this meeting got completely out of hand.

Quicker than you could say "koinonia," we were in the midst of a knock-down, drag-out battle. The group quickly divided itself into two battalions: the 100-chair battalion and the 120-chair battalion. Each battalion had a leader, and the battle was joined.

Voices got loud.

Passions rose.

Moderators quaked.

We must've argued about the number of chairs for at least an hour. Eventually, we took a vote, and one side or the other won (I can't remember which), and people went home either sad or glad, depending on which battalion they were in.

If I didn't know the Time Paradox before then, I certainly learned it that night. The Time Paradox says, *The less important the issue, the more time you will spend on it.* It's a paradox more prevalent in the church than we like to admit.

Concerning the Time Paradox, I offer you three quick observations.

First, in spite of our wishes to the contrary, the church is an institution and exhibits the flaws inherent in all institutions. It pains me to type that sentence. I've spent most of my ministry denying the institutional nature of the church. I like to think of the church as somehow different than other institutions, and I suppose in some ways it is. But on my more honest days, I know the church *is* an institution and that it's governed by all of those weird laws that become part and parcel of any institutional system.

There's Soper's Law: *Any bureaucracy designed to enhance efficiency is immediately indistinguishable from its predecessor.*

There's Owen's Theory of Organizational Deviance: *Every organization has an allotted number of positions to be filled by misfits.* And its corollary, *Once a misfit leaves, another will be recruited.*

There's Mollison's Bureaucracy Hypothesis: *If an idea can survive a bureaucratic review and be implemented, it wasn't worth doing.*

There's Sweeney's Law: *The length of a progress report is inversely proportional to the amount of progress.*

There's Jacobson's Law: *The less work an organization produces, the more frequently it reorganizes.*

And there's Cohn's Law: *In any bureaucracy, paperwork increases as you spend more and more time reporting on the less and less you are doing. Stability is achieved when you spend all of your time reporting on the nothing you are doing.*[1]

Any person involved in institutional life has to laugh at those laws, but it's a nervous laughter because they're so true. And the church is certainly not exempt from them. The Time Paradox—*The less important the issue, the more time you will spend on it*—is true for the church, just as it's true for all institutions. Chances are good we'll have to endure the agony of this paradox all of our days.

That means long meetings focused on minutiae. It means committees that spend their time on piddling concerns. It means church business meetings spent arguing about trivia. And it means trips home from church dreaming of becoming a forest ranger. We're caught in the web of the *institutional* church, with all of the joys and miseries inherent in institutional life.

Second, be aware of the Time Paradox, and do your best to keep the church focused on the things that matter. Go back to that maintenance/ministry distinction I drew earlier in the book. It's our job as pastors to keep the church focused on the right side of that distinction. Granted, some maintenance has to be done, but primarily a church is about ministry. We're in the business of touching people's lives for Jesus' sake.

But the maintenance tasks can become all-consuming. If a church doesn't watch it, it can become focused primarily on nonessentials. Church becomes an exercise in triviality, and the Time Paradox reigns supreme in almost every gathering. Much time is spent on little of consequence.

Here's a laundry list of "necessary activities" that could keep a church occupied for a long time. The church could even delude itself into thinking these tasks are the reasons it exists. But the more any church focuses on these activities, the more operative the Time Paradox becomes:

- Regularly rework and revise the church bylaws.
- Regularly rework and revise staff job descriptions.
- Create and oversee numerous church policies and procedures.
- Spend months talking about vision statements, mission statements, and long-range plans.
- Make sure committees meet regularly, even if they don't have anything to do.
- Focus on your facilities—replacing the carpet in the sanctuary, redoing the parking lot, adding on to the library, etc.
- Concentrate on appearances and image—redesign your visitor's cards, stationery, bulletin, newsletter, and any other church promotional material.
- Focus on the staff—evaluating the staff, doing surveys about the staff, getting the staff to fill out all kinds of forms, suggesting improvements to the staff.
- Survey the church on a regular basis to determine needs and future ministries.
- Study other churches to see what they're doing to grow and be effective.

There, that should do it. That's enough to keep us busy for the next year or so. And if our church decides to adopt that laundry list of necessary activities, our agenda is set. We're off and running. Our facilities will be immaculate, our staff accountable and trained, our documents flawless and up-to-date, and our image impeccable.

But the sick will go unvisited, the hungry unfed, the homeless left in the cold, and the spiritual wanderers lost in confusion. In doing those *good* maintenance activities, we must leave untended the *better* ministry activities.

Whatever else we pastors do, we must keep the church focused on what matters. We must keep people focused on ministry, not maintenance.

Third, the most effective way to thwart the Time Paradox in the church is to manage your personal time well. As a pastor, I'm to use my influence to keep the church focused on what matters, but that's not my first responsibility. My first responsibility is to keep my own life focused on what matters. The best way to keep the church out of the frustrating grasp of the Time Paradox is to stay out of it myself.

That means I must spend most of my time doing ministry, not maintenance. I must consciously choose to pray, study, write, do pastoral care, plan worship, and keep myself attentive to God. If I can keep my personal priorities straight, I can do a better job of helping the church keep its priorities straight.

There's no way to avoid all maintenance tasks, of course. As I said, the church *is* an institution, and institutions must be maintained. I'll spend some days attending budget meetings, doing staff reviews, or trying to get my computer running, but those days shouldn't dominate my schedule. Not if I have my priorities straight. Primarily, I'm here to help build a kingdom, not maintain an institution.

I might say, parenthetically, that I've grown to appreciate the people in my church who gravitate toward maintenance duties. Some people don't mind at all revising the bylaws or writing new financial policies. In fact, they relish those chores. Instead of being critical of these people, I've come to appreciate them greatly. Their presence means I don't have to do those things! Maybe God, in divine wisdom, has blessed every church with people who will take care of the necessary maintenance details so that the rest of the church can get on with ministry. Let's take it a step further and say that maintenance might be some people's ministry.

My role as pastor is not to criticize people who maintain the institutional church. My role is to keep the bigger picture before the church and to make sure I'm modeling a life that is attentive to the spiritual.

Leaders, in any kind of institution, must know where they're going and what their priorities are. Then and only then will the institution they lead stay on course.

Be forewarned, though. Even if you do that, even if you keep your personal priorities straight and even if you try to keep the church out of the clutches of the Time Paradox, you won't always succeed. You'll inevitably have exasperating business meetings like the one I described. You'll attend countless committee meetings where nothing of substance is accomplished. And you'll have times when you have to vent to your husband or wife because of the craziness of it all.

I read once about a priest who had the duty of listening to the confessions of an order of nuns. Day after day, this priest sat in his confession booth, while a parade of nuns came to confess their sins. Someone asked him what it was like to hear the confessions of nuns all day. His answer was classic. He said it was like "being stoned to death with popcorn."

All too often, that's the plight of the modern pastor too. We get stoned to death with popcorn. We get inundated with little annoyances and "maintenance issues" that, over time, sap our strength and drain our joy. The dastardly Time Paradox sucks the life out of us and makes us feel we're investing too much of our life in trivia.

But once we acknowledge the Time Paradox, we're on the way to dealing with it. We can begin to do what we can, both individually and corporately, to spend our time wisely, focusing on substantive issues.

We're also realistic and candid enough to know, though, that somewhere in the near future is a knockdown, drag-out business meeting over some eternally significant issue, like folding chairs for the fellowship hall.

---

[1] All of these laws are from Arthur Bloch, *The Complete Murphy's Law* (Los Angeles: Price Stern Sloan, 1990).

The Attitude Paradox

*Only pastors who are having fun
can seriously proclaim the gospel.*

Back in chapter 2, when I was pontificating about the Calendar Paradox, I used a quote from Robert Capon that might have seemed a little shocking. I quote it again here to lead you to consider the Attitude Paradox: "Every call from God, whether into some dull line of paid work or into an excursion from such work, is a call into play—into *fun,* if you will. If you turn it into mere labor, or into a career, or into a way of making money, it will either blow up in your face, or burn you out—or both."[1]

As I ponder my own years as a pastor, I think Capon is on to something. I think God calls pastors to have fun. In fact, I believe the Attitude Paradox reigns supreme over the pastor's life: *Only pastors who are having fun can seriously proclaim the gospel.*

Even as I write that paradox, though, I can hear voices of protest swelling around me. The protests, if I hear them correctly, go something like this:

"Fun!? Fun!? You think a pastor is supposed to have fun? How can it be fun to stand at the graveside of a baby? How can it be fun to deal with petty, mean-spirited people day after day? How can it be fun to have to speak a word of eternal significance Sunday after Sunday? How can it be fun to be trapped in an institution that seems to be going nowhere fast? How can it be fun to see attendance and offerings spiraling downward? You call that fun?"

"I'm well acquainted with Scripture, and I don't recall one passage advocating that pastors, or Christians in general, have fun. Do you think Jesus' life was fun? Do you think Paul had fun in prison? Do you suppose the Christian martyrs were having fun? This notion of pastors having fun sounds more like secular gospel than biblical gospel. As I read it, the biblical gospel is more about persevering than partying."

"Your suggestion that pastors should have more fun sounds good, but it doesn't square with the Bible. And it doesn't square with my experience either."

I understand completely. Truth to tell, those swelling voices of protest aren't just around me. They're *within* me. I know that the life of a pastor isn't always a picnic. I know about hostile business meetings, cantankerous church members, sagging attendance and offerings, and days when going to church is absolute torture. I know. I've been there and done that.

And I know, too, what the Bible says. I know, and have quoted often, those passages about putting your hand to the plow and never looking back. Running with perseverance the race set before us. Jesus enduring the agony of the cross. Paul pressing on in the midst of suffering. I know. I know.

But still, I sense Capon is right. The call of God is supposed to be a call to *fun*, to a life of passion and purpose, to a life of delight and fascination. When I look back on my life as a pastor, I see that the times I've been the best pastor are the times I've laughed the most, hung the loosest, and tried to enjoy the ride, the times I've not taken myself or my job too seriously. Paradoxically, I've been able to proclaim the gospel most seriously when I've had the most fun.

So, as I angle toward the close of this book, let me offer you a few reflections on the Attitude Paradox. I do so with the fond hope that all of us pastors can find a way to have more fun.

First, the Attitude Paradox is true for all people, not just pastors. Tom Peters, in *The Pursuit of WOW!*, writes, "Business, life itself, is . . . hard work if you wanna be good at it. Actually, that's precisely wrong. Business ceases to be work when you're chasing a dream that has engorged you. ("Work should be more fun than fun."—Noel Coward.) And if the passion isn't there, then biotech and plumbing will be equal drags."[2]

It's true for biotech experts, plumbers, and pastors: The people with the passion, the people who are having fun, are the ones who do the best job. The Attitude Paradox reigns supreme over every human endeavor. Only those who are having fun can expect to succeed.

Only musicians who are having fun can seriously play music. Only parents who are having fun can seriously raise their children. Only youth ministers who are having fun can seriously relate to teenagers. Only baseball players who are having fun can seriously improve their game. And so on, ad infinitum. The Attitude Paradox can be applied across the board.

Second, we pastors can start having fun when we experience the good news we preach. It's one thing, of course, to say we want to have fun in our work as pastors. It's another thing altogether to *have* fun, to be delighted with our work. How do we pull that off? How do we pastors learn to have fun?

It begins, I believe, with a clear understanding of the good news we claim to believe. It begins when we get it clear in our own minds and hearts that we're loved and treasured by God just as we are—without ministerial success, without a mega-church, without great oratorical skills, without strong leadership instincts, without all the answers to people's problems. We're held in the grace of God, in spite of ourselves. We're free. But pastors tend to be the most un-free people in the world. We who preach grace loudest shun it most. Though we'd never articulate it, our credo is: "Grace for everybody else, but Law for me." Maybe the reason we preach grace so loudly is that we ourselves want it so desperately.

More than thirty years ago, Karl Olsson wrote a magnificent book titled *Come to the Party*. It should be required reading for all pastors because it details Olsson's search for "the blessing." He was a pastor, professor, and college president, but like the elder brother he never felt secure in the Father's love. He felt himself to be among "the unblessed," those who strive and struggle to make it with God but never get God's favor. Olsson feels that most pastors number themselves among "the unblessed."

Then his life changed:

> Some time in the summer of 1967, [I came] face to face with the real me and suddenly discovered the simple but overwhelming fact I had preached and written about for thirty years—that we are justified by faith alone and not by works, "lest any man should boast." What this meant for *me*, quite practically, was that God had already accepted the real *me* in Christ and that it was O.K. to be that *me*. I did not have to overlay that *me* with any sweat-soaked slave shirt of my own. I did not have to be a professional prelate, preacher, president, pundit, professor, Protestant, or anything else to make it with God. I didn't have to be eaten up by malarial mosquitoes, slog through mud, contract dysentery, translate the Bible, swallow the mutterings and up-tight rantings of paranoids, study the next move on the great religio-political chessboard, win every argument and every tennis game, speak to 50,000 people, read the Bible through eighteen times, pray for twenty-four hours at a stretch, balance the budget, be listed in *Who's Who*, empty bedpans, bridge the generation gap, be bored, be insulted, be tense, be tired—I did not, praise God in the highest, need to *do* any of these or *be* any of these in order to make it with God. I was free to be me and to be human.[3]

If we ever get to that place—the place where grace is not just preached but experienced—we'll be on the way to having fun in the ministry. Because then our "success" doesn't have anything to do with the size of our church. Because then our ego won't be shattered by criticism. Because then we'll be held in the delightful, fascinating grip of a good God who wonders why we get so uptight about trifles.

If we ever have an experience like Olsson's, we'll start having fun. And we'll start preaching and ministering like never before. For the first time, we'll be pastors who know how fun the party really is.

Third, the Attitude Paradox gives us a needed paradigm shift. It makes us pastors look at our calling in a whole new way.

When I was a boy, I had aspirations of being a high jumper. Just about every day, I practiced at school and then in my backyard. I used the "scissors technique," where I hurled one leg over the bar and then the other leg over the bar. It was one of two techniques all high jumpers used in those days. The other technique was the "western roll," where the jumper rolled over the bar. But in both techniques, the jumper's legs went over the bar first.

Then along came a high jumper named Dick Fosbury. He had a wildly unorthodox style that came to be known as "The Fosbury Flop." He sailed over the bar head and back first, with his legs trailing behind. No one had ever seen such a bizarre way to high jump. At first, people scoffed. But when Dick Fosbury won the gold medal in the 1968 Olympics, people stopped scoffing.

Suddenly, "The Fosbury Flop" was all the rage. People everywhere started using it, and today every self-respecting high jumper in the world is a "flopper." Fosbury gave the world of high jumping a paradigm shift.

Something like that needs to happen in the world of pastors and Christian leaders. Right now, pastors are using the "perseverance technique." We grit our teeth and try to be faithful. We drag ourselves to church to preach another sermon or attend another committee meeting. The world's concept of the pastor as a beleaguered figure stricken by the flu-bug for two weeks is pretty much on target. We're tired, run down, burned out, bereft of laughter and joy. It's the way pastors have always "gone over the bar," and it seemingly has produced some pretty fine jumpers.

But we need a Fosbury paradigm shift to take place in the ministerial world. We need a few pastors to try the "enjoyment technique." We need pastors who are having fun, who enjoy what they're doing, who have so experienced grace themselves that they can share it with others. We need pastors who are tantalizingly alive, who are real and human.

Earlier in this book, I mentioned an uncle who wrote me that I was "stuck with the way I was glued together." That uncle, Glen Edwards, was a pastor for years, a voracious reader, a genuine human being, and a person who knew exactly where I was coming from. He was, for me, the definition of "a kindred spirit." Whenever I got depressed about something in the church, I could call or write Uncle Glen and find an understanding soul.

Once, early in my ministry, I wrote him a letter complaining about a number of things. I questioned my place in the church, wondered if I wouldn't be happier doing something else. I grumped and groaned in the letter that I didn't "fit" in the church and would never be a successful pastor.

In response, he wrote a letter I've saved in a stack of letters he sent me over the years. He wrote, "Your temperament, personality, style, etc. will preclude your being a 'successful pastor' and guarantee that you will be an authentic human being. The latter, for all its discomfort and misfitness, is preferable to the former."

As usual, Uncle Glen was right. Better to be an authentic human being than a successful pastor. Better to be an ecclesiastical misfit than a denominational clone. The new paradigm calls for pastors who are *people* first—real, live human beings who doubt, cry, laugh, and display all kinds of funny eccentricities.

What I've tried to do in this book is remind all of us who are pastors that we're in a fun, confusing, confounding, delightful, paradoxical profession. The twenty-one paradoxes I've mentioned are probably just the tip of the iceberg. I challenge you to add to the list.

But don't make the pastoral life black and white, void of intrigue, lacking in mystery. Don't reduce our calling to X's and O's, point and principles. What we're about is richer and deeper than that.

I close with a quote from Charles Handy in his book, *The Age of Paradox*:

Living with paradox is not comfortable or easy. It can be like walking in a dark wood on a moonlit night. It is an eerie and, at times, frightening experience. All sense of direction is lost; trees and bushes crowd in on you; wherever you step, you bump into another obstacle; every noise and rustle is magnified; there is a whiff of danger; it seems safer to stand still than to move. Come the dawn, however, and your path is clear; the noises are now the songs of birds and the rustle in the undergrowth is only scuttling rabbits; trees define the path instead of blocking it. The wood is a different place. So will our world look different and less frightening if we can bring light to the paradoxes.[4]

I've tried. Keep the faith. And have fun.

[1] Robert Capon, *Health, Money, & Love* (Grand Rapids: Eerdmans, 1990), 143.

[2] Tom Peters, *The Pursuit of WOW!* (New York: Vintage Books, 1994), 22.

[3] Karl Olsson, *Come to the Party* (Waco TX: Word Books, 1972), 46-47.

[4] Charles Handy, *The Age of Paradox* (Boston: Harvard Business School, 1994), 14.